D1536902

LEGS GET
LED ASTRAY

CHLOE CALDWELL

Future Tense Books
portland, oregon

Legs Get Led Astray
Chloe Caldwell

This is a work of non-fiction. In some essays, names have
been changed.

ISBN 978-1-892061-42-3

Future Tense Books
PO Box 42416
Portland, OR 97242
www.futuretensebooks.com

CONTENTS

Kids get lost, lambs out wandering, bigger, blacker things come calling from outside a tiny garden, somebody once laid their hearts on and kids get lost, and kids get broken, diaries get found and opened. Their legs get led astray and then they lie inside some secret place where the sun looks in the open ceiling, kids grow up and kids stop feeling, kids then feel adult and face away.

— Will Sheff of Okkervil River, "Last Love Song For Now"

BARNEY

I wanted to be on the TV show *Barney and Friends*. I wanted to be famous. I thought if I got on *Barney* then I would be famous. Jesus, that's weird. That I wanted that. I just wanted to be one of those kids. They were happy. I was happy too. They could sing. So could I. I think I was too old to be watching *Barney*. I was like seven or eight. Wikipedia says it's a show for kids 1-8 years old, so I guess I made the cut. Who comes up with those cuts anyway? Wikipedia says that Barney "conveys learning through songs and small dance routines with a friendly, optimistic attitude." Barney is a total optimist. It's why I liked him.

I wanted to be Little Orphan Annie. I belted along to the record in the living room and I knew every word to "It's A Hard Knock Life." I wanted red hair. I wanted freckles. I also wanted glasses and braces. I got a kick out of yelling: "No one cares for you—a smidge—when you're in an orphanage!"

I wanted to be a tap dancer. I wanted to be Shirley Temple. When I was five, my dad told me a true story about a ninety-something-year-old man whose house he was doing carpentry on. One day he couldn't find the man and when he found him he was in his yard tap dancing on a piece of plywood. I was moved by the story and thought it sounded really fun so my dad cut me a 4'x4' square piece of plywood and I wore shoes that weren't real tap shoes and tapped. I put on shows for my babysitters. I remember singing, "You're a good ship, Lollipop" to a boy babysitter and he laughed his ass off. I charged my babysitters fifty cents to watch me. Funny, I was more into making money then than I am now. One day I was spinning in tights on the wooden square and I did a face plant. Which wasn't all bad—I'd been born with a small cyst on my nose and when I fell, it popped. I still had to have an operation though. They gave me anesthesia and the last thing I remember is the doctor asking me what kinds of ice cream I liked and I said strawberry.

Around that same time I wanted my name to be Anna. I changed it the year I was five. I jumped off couches trying to fly like Peter Pan and announcing: "I'm Anna." It didn't stick.

I wanted to be in *A Chorus Line*. My family had the tape and the record. I knew every word from "Singular Sensation" to "Tits and Ass." My favorite was the song, "At The Ballet." A girl sings about her dysfunctional parents and how she was only happy at ballet class. My favorite part:

> *I did have a fantastic fantasy life. I used to dance around the living room with my arms up like this. My fantasy was that my dad was an Indian chief and he'd look at me and say, 'Maggie, do you want to dance?' And I'd say, 'Daddy...I would loooooove to dance.'*

It's interesting that I loved that part because I didn't have a fantasy life; I had a great childhood. I pretty much *did* dance around the living room 24/7 and the living room was full of love. Sometimes I think I wanted my life to be more tragic than it was, as if I was gliding along too easily.

On videotape, I'm always spinning and curtsying and singing the same lyrics over and over until eventually my mother says, "Okay Clo. Okay Clo—take a bow, Clo. Take a bow, *now*, Chloe." My father begins to laugh.

I wanted to be a ballerina. I wanted to dance *en pointe*. I was really into this series of books about a group of girlfriends, by Emily Costello: *Becky at the Barre. Jillian on Her Toes. Katie's Last Class.* I read them and re-read them. I liked Katie the best, the fuck-up. The girl who stopped going to class. I could relate. I quit ballet.

I wanted to be a singer. I took voice lessons above a Chinese food restaurant after school. The teacher played piano poorly and had long blonde hair and a horse-like mouth. I loved her. The first song we did was "Second Hand Rose" and the second was "My Boyfriend's Back." Years later I went to a voice and guitar camp for a summer in Connecticut and fell in love with a boy that played shred guitar and my vocal teacher, Django.

I wanted to be Maria. My family had the *West Side Story* record. I replayed the part where Tony gets shot, while Maria sings: "There's a place for us…a time and place for us" and then breaks into hysterics and yells "No!" Some of the gang walk near but Maria yells "Don't…you…touch him!"

I bawled. I practiced it over and over until I had her Spanish tongue down and my sobs exactly aligned with hers. I wanted a passionate relationship like that. I wanted to scream and sob over someone's dead body.

Back when I called myself Anna, I'd also wanted to be Maria. I pranced around the house in leggings and bracelets and barrettes and sang, "I feel pretty, I feel pretty, aren't I pretty and witty and gay?" Until the "Take a Bow" was enforced.

When I was home alone at night I turned the lights low and sang my heart out. I performed facing the big window framed like a tic-tac-toe board because it made it look like there were three of me. That way I could pretend I was on Broadway, and the girls to my left and right were not me and we were dancing in sync like a choreographed routine.

I wanted to be Dusty Springfield. My dad and I drove to a wedding and on the way we listened to "I Only Want to Be with You" on the tape deck and I wouldn't listen to any other song for weeks. On the way home from the wedding, we listened to the song more, but I had a stomachache because

I'd snuck off and ate bright red berries, the ones meant only for birds.

I also wanted to be a Marvelette. I wanted to wear a green sequined dress and sing "Mr. Postman."

I was cast as Lucy in *You're a Good Man, Charlie Brown* when I was in fifth grade. I had a lot of solos. It was sort of my big break.

I wanted to sing opera. I studied and performed Italian arias. Then my batshit vocal teacher told me my larynx was kind of messed up and that I should go to a doctor. My mom took me and to this day says she is amazed at how calm I was when they sent the mirror on the wire down my nose and to my throat. She thought I was going to scream or something but I didn't. Nothing ended up being wrong with my larynx but I got to miss some mornings of school to go to some speech therapist.

I wanted to be Scout from *To Kill a Mockingbird.* I auditioned for the part at the Capital Repertory Theatre in Albany. I read a monologue. I knew on the drive there that if I got the part my social life would be gone. I knew that it was a decision I should make: acting or friends. I didn't get the part.

I wanted to be Mariah Carey. Sometimes people told me I looked like her. I had a round face and long curly hair. There was an MTV special on her, where she visited her old high school and I taped it on VHS and watched it every Saturday morning. I sang her songs about self-esteem in the living room.

I wanted to be a rock star. I wanted to be Gwen Stefani. A front woman. I rocked dark lipstick on pale skin and I think I even wore a bindhi. I got my belly button pierced and sprayed Sun-In in my hair. At the school talent show I sang, "I Want You to Want Me" by Cheap Trick. My best friend played bass. We had one more gig in the summer and we played "Just a Girl" by No Doubt. I stole some of No Doubt's melodies and wrote my own words to them and claimed them as my own. I recorded the No Doubt *Behind the Music* on VHS and watched it after school and cried when Gwen talked about her breakup with Tony, the bass player.

I wanted to be a hip-hop dancer and I wanted to be tan. I went tanning every day after school. It was only five bucks a pop back then, in 2002. My parents were separated at this point and I didn't have a license yet. My dad drove me to my hip-hop class on Tuesday nights and we listened to Fly92 on the way.

I was in a few more plays after that but then I started smoking marijuana, and I wanted to be even more things.

THE LEGENDARY LUKE

Bright red and yellow Strand shopping bags caught my eye through the window of my mom's green Honda, as she pulled up our driveway. It was one of the first afternoons in April with no rain, and I was sitting outside on our stoop with the daffodils and mosquitoes, reading *Valley of the Dolls*, a birthday gift from my brother.

My mom was returning from a weekend in the city to help Trev move out of Bedford-Stuyvesant and into his new, yet old, railroad apartment in the heart of Williamsburg.

We were hardly inside our house with the heavy bags before my mother began describing Trev's friends to me. He'd been working in the basement of the Strand bookstore for over a year. She'd done quite a bit of bargain book hunting with some help from the basement boys.

I learned that Eric from the dirty south of Texas was enveloped in tattoos. He drove the Strand van in addition to working in the basement. The face of his dead mother covered one of his thick biceps in black ink.

"Of all the tattoos I've seen in my life, that is the only one that's ever made any sense to me," my mom sighed. "It broke my heart."

"*Wow*. What else? Who else?" I pried. I loved getting details on my older brother's New York City life.

"Luke—the guys called him The *Legendary* Luke—he was the wild and most confident one. Mr. Cool, with a nose ring and long scraggly hair." I sat down on the couch. I've always carried an affinity for the dark ones.

"Sam is skinny and tall," she continued. "He's kind of timid like Trev and really dorky-looking but cute, with glasses." I'd later notice that what she'd described was every other guy I'd meet from the Strand.

New York City was a fictional place that spring day while we sat alone in our little living room in the woods. My mom and I were addicted to *Sex and the City* at the time, renting it weekly from the video store, and one afternoon the phone rang while we were watching it. It was my brother calling from Union Square on his lunch break. I could hear all the noise from New York in the background. "What are you doing?" He asked me. "Watching *Sex and the City* with mom," I said. He scoffed and said, "Why?"

Visualizing all these guys that worked with my twenty-three-year-old brother at the Strand and romanticizing about living in the city gave me something to think about. In my reality, I lived in Upstate New York, in an uninspired cardboard box town. My free time was dedicated to my vanilla boyfriend, Adam. I'd always been envious of Trevor. Older brothers are always doing something more interesting than you (backpacking through Mexico, hitchhiking around Finland, moving to New York City) and they are ruthless about letting you know it.

My mom and I were thrilled because making friends had never been in Trevor's nature. I played the part of the pothead prom queen while Trev was the scholar and severe loner. At the Strand bookstore though, his own kith and kin surrounded him. Trev was popular for the first time in his life.

I checked his friends out on Myspace. Just seeing their locations screaming, "NEW YORK CITY, New York," and "BROOKLYN! New York," deemed them heroes in my opinion. The Legendary Luke was especially rousing, with his headline: "Breaking hearts and faces," and his default photo reminding me of the Elliott Smith "Either/Or" album cover. I wanted badly to be a part of this special thing that Trev seemed to be implicated in, just two hours down the state. He'd been egging me on to move to the city for months, and I visited frequently, but I was preoccupied popping Percocet pills and procrastinating moving in with Adam.

In May, Trev's depressed roommate disappeared back to her home in Connecticut, with no plans of returning to the city.

Trev called me while I was at work at my dad's guitar store:

"Hello, this is Musica."

"Hey, Clo, 'sup? Do you still want to move to the city?"

"Well yeah, but…"

He cut me off: "Okay, you can move in June first. It'll be six-hundred dollars rent plus another six-hundred dollars for the security deposit. Try and convince Dad to help you. Then pay him back."

It was May 25th. I had five days to work overtime for my dad and with little success I tried to stop blowing every penny of my paycheck up my nose. I assured Adam that it would just be for three months, just for the summer. But we knew I wasn't coming back.

I swallowed a Vicodin and then slept with the sun on my face while my mom drove me down to the city on the 2nd of June. I'd been up until dawn, drinking Budweiser and snorting lines with Adam and my friends. Going through the motions of moving had been a rushed blur: packing my clothes and photos, writing guilt-induced goodbye letters to Adam, writing out six-hundred dollar checks. But at three in the afternoon, the sun became too yellow and too hard to ignore, awaking me on the Williamsburg Bridge. I opened my eyes just in time to read "Brooklyn—Like No Other Place in the World," and the vim and vigor of the filthy water and brick apartment buildings and plants on fire escapes and men on construction sites and clear broad sky exhilarated my body. It was then that a skittish feeling struck my core, warning me that I was really *going*. This skittish feeling lingered inside of me for months.

I hadn't grasped how confined I'd felt until a noise of relief escaped my mouth, surprising me as I walked down North Sixth Street. I aggressively pressed the bell to #199, thankful that this was going to be my future home. When Trev answered the door he smiled and squinted into the sun, and said, "Hey, roomie!" But after he sized me up in my striped tank top, headband, ripped jeans, and Brooklyn Industries messenger bag, he grimaced and said, "God. You look like such a hipster already."

Bags were unpacked and my room—mattress on the floor and flowered curtain for a door—was set up. My brother criticized my long plastic shoe holder and compulsive shoe buying habit. It didn't complement his neurotic collection of Nabokov books. "Yup," he sneered, "my friends are definitely going to make fun of you for this." He hammered it into the wall nonetheless. *A Million Little Pieces* by James Frey was unpacked along with my other books. Trev noticed it before I had a chance to cover it up. "That's just embarrassing. Hide your books when my friends come over."

Trev and I walked the six blocks down to Fix Café, discussing what floor I'd be assigned to if I ended up working at the Strand. "You'd probably be an Art Floor girl," he said, as I followed him into Fix.

The Legendary Luke Young himself was in attendance, on the couch. Mr. Cool, as my mother had called him, wore a Tom Waits T-shirt and was furiously scribbling in his journal. Introductions were made, and Trev asked, "Luke, what floor would Chloe work on if she worked at Strand?"

"Two," he responded, not even looking up, though I'd felt him watching me as I walked in. Now he was looking into his vodka and cranberry juice instead.

"See?" Trev turned to me.

Coming up for air from a long sip on his straw, Luke added: "But whatever you do, *don't* work at the Strand! That place is *screwed*." I pledged to Luke as well as myself that I wouldn't work there. I'd find my own niche.

We had a drink with him, and then Trev and I left to go see Antony and the Johnsons at the Bowery Ballroom. While the L train sped under the water, I did my best to nonchalantly ask Trev about Luke's history. When he finished talking, I concluded that it sounded like Luke had had plenty of girlfriends. "I guess he has." Trev said. He considered my comment more and added, "Yeah, stay away from him!" We both laughed.

I met tall Sam in the basement of the Strand the next day, when I took a breather from handing out my resumes in the East Village. "This is my sister, Chloe," Trev said, and Sam's head whipped around, his jaw agape, a flicker of joy noticeable in his brown eyes behind his glasses. Sam carries a rare appreciation around with him and pulls it out for small moments, like meeting his friend's sister.

The ominous 6/6/06 fell on a Tuesday, and Trev decided to throw a party in its honor. I arrived after everyone else. I'd been applying for jobs around Williamsburg. Everyone in my apartment but me was a Strand employee. Initiation into what my existence would become for the next few years.

Eric was identifiable from my mom's tattoo description. I saw him smoking cigarettes with some guys on the fire escape. He looked approachable in his plaid shirt and large silver belt buckle that read "ART," so I crawled out the window to join him.

"Eric, right? I'm Chloe, Trevor's sister," I said. He was straight away warm and kept making noises of affirmation while I spoke about how I'd just moved in from upstate and was looking for a job.

"Mm hmm, mm hmm," he repeated and repeated while I spoke. I thought it was strange that his eyes were twitching and his head nodded unrelentingly.

Trevor and my mom had both failed to let me know that Eric had a harsh case of Tourette's syndrome. Months later I learned that he'd been doing a shit ton of cocaine that night, amplifying his ticks all the more. I was twenty. Just assumed he'd been agreeing with everything I said.

From the fire escape, I peered into the bathroom window and caught an eyeful of Luke sitting on the toilet. He was wearing a psychedelic silk shirt that accentuated his rich scarlet hair. Freshly dyed. A girl was standing over him and I could tell from their motions they were arguing. When they came out, Luke climbed onto the fire escape. "Heeeyyyyy Chloeee! When did *you* get here? Hey, how do you get your hair so curly like that?" he asked, tousling my hair and getting comfortable beside me.

Eric and Luke broke down to me how the Strand operated.

"They put the intellectuals like us in the basement. It's like we're overly smart and below good-looking, so they hide us down there," Eric said.

"Yeah, and everyone wants to fuck the Art Floor girls," Luke said. "Anyone left gets put on the main floor—the generics," he shrugged. I didn't bring up that he'd pinned me for an Art Floor girl, but it was on my mind.

Luke and I sat shoulder to shoulder on the fire escape in the black June night. We passed his Tropicana bottle back and forth, taking turns swigging the vodka and cranberry juice. It was so acidic, each swallow scorching in my stomach.

"I love your dangerous dark eyes."

"My eyes are green," I told him.

Pause.

"They're dark to me. *You're* dark to me," he countered.

I was flattered.

The three-in-the-morning party peak hit and, then when five A.M. neared, the festivities began to die. People started to head for the door, mumbling about work the next day or catching the train. I was fixing myself another drink when I heard Luke say, "Whose shoes are these?" I looked over my shoulder and he was near the shoe rack, fondling one of my black flats.

"Probably Chloe's?" Trev shrugged.

"Figures. Fucking poser," Luke snapped.

I froze. Earlier in the night he'd been pleasant. I was uncertain if this was friendly banter, or if he just thought I was a huge fraud.

Eric, Luke, Trev and I sat on the wooden floor in the unlit living room, still steadily drinking. Luke sang his apparently notorious song about working at the Strand. He crooned quirky lyrics while strumming dramatic minor chords on Trevor's guitar. Everyone knew all of the words and sang along:

Art Floor Girls, do you wanna discuss art?
We can laugh and sound smart, and fall in love.
Art Floor Girls, do you wanna discuss Goya?
Or does my greasy hair annoy ya?
Art Floor Girls.
I work in the basement—well what can you do…
But Art Floor Girls, Goddamn I can make it for YOUUUU!

My brother and Eric had already left for the Strand when I woke up hung over in the morning. Luke had the day off and was asleep on the futon. I was still jobless. I felt anxious, a bit afraid to be alone with Luke. I toyed around in the bright white kitchen, pouring quarter-full beer bottles down the drain and wiping the table down with a sponge. I picked up a Marlboro red pack off the table. Shook it. No cigs. Trashed it.

I got bored after a while and went onto the fire escape to marinate in summer, which seemed to have happened overnight. The crown of my head ached from last night's liquor, and the unforgiving sun didn't help, but it was just my fifth morning waking up in New York City—I was still so high on my new environment that everything felt good.

Luke rose a bit later and climbed out next to me while saying, "Morning *little sister*." His hard eyes were softer today. He handed me a cigarette and I noticed his nails bitten to the quick.

"Your hands look like mine," I told him.

"I'm aware," he said, reaching to light the Marlboro dangling from my mouth. He watched me inhale and exhale for a moment. "*Poser*," he nudged me and cracked a smile. I felt more comfortable with him now, sharing the nail-biting neurosis.

The heat pushed us back inside. Luke dug around for his drugs for twenty minutes while I watched from the kitchen table, tired.

"That's like one-hundred dollars worth of dope down the drain," he stated, irritated.

"What do you keep it in?" I finally thought to ask him.

"A Marlboro cigarette pack."

Oh. Oops.

I walked over to the trashcan and rummaged through to retrieve the Marlboro pack that I hadn't known had been holding a tiny bag of heroin. He smiled, his eyes mischievous. "You're a con artist," he smirked at me. I started arguing that I hadn't done it on purpose and he interrupted: "Just like me," he said, smug.

We sat talking for a while across the table from each other. We realized we identified with one another more than we'd initially thought. We were both from small towns, we'd both gone to school for human services, wanting to be substance abuse counselors. On the contrary, we both did drugs. I was coming off a year-and-a-half binge of painkillers and Luke was trying to supplement his boredom by being an aspiring junky. I tried persuading him to share the dope with me.

He was hesitant but I talked him into it and we did some lines of the brown sugary-tasting heroin, making us giddy and relaxed. While the conversation kept flowing, the kitchen windows overflowed with sun and smoke from our cigarettes. We were listening to Coco Rosie; we were falling all over each other laughing half the time.

"I'm so glad you moved to New York!" Luke exclaimed.

"Everyone else here is so fucking uptight. Plus," he added, "I needed a new muse. My songwriting has been suffering." He looked at me then with an authority that challenged me to not find him mesmerizing, even when he said something offensive.

The moment I decided to put Luke inside of me was contemplative. I was conscious of the fact that he was a little insane, that he was my brother's good friend, that I was playing with fire, that he'd given me heroin. I looked down at him, squirming with his eyes squeezed shut in his psychedelic shirt. His dyed hair spread out on the maroon sheets, almost the same color. I looked up at myself in the mirror my brother and I had found on the street with the huge crack down the middle. I stared at my reflection. My hipbones were prominent. I'd let a hopeful hairdresser chop off inches of my blonde hair at the 6/6/06 party, and I wasn't used to it yet. Black lace bra. Three necklaces. I guided him inside of me.

Many Junes later now, there are certain days of the month when the sun will leak through the window of the kitchen, merge with cigarette or candle smoke in a particular way, and it will remind me of that morning.

"You two are going to eat each other *alive*," Eric had to talk straight into my ear, to be heard over *Time of the Season* by The Zombies. We were in the Lower East Side at the Skinny Bar a few nights after 6/6/06 where he and Luke were DJ-ing.

"Luke is always trying to do some Kerouac/Bukowski bullshit." We were upstairs, in the DJ booth, and I gazed down over the ramp at Luke. He was dancing wearing a dashiki. (No one ever knew what kind of statement he was trying to make with his shirt choices.) One of his arms was slung around my brother's neck and a drink was in his hand. He was the only one dancing. He looked up at Eric and I and winked. "And it seems like *you* get off on excitement," Eric said, watching Luke and I exchange secret smiles.

"Yeah, right, that's like the *furthest* thing away from what I'm trying to do," Luke defended himself, when I relayed Eric's theory to him. "*Especially* the Kerouac part, man, that's not even obscure enough for me! Eric's just jealous because I found you, and we're *wonderful* for each other."

Fortunately I found a job at an Israeli café in Williamsburg, so I didn't have to piggyback my brother and work at the Strand. The café was just a few blocks from my apartment, and if it weren't for the Strand, I'd rarely have gone into Manhattan at all. I poured iced coffee and served hummus and pita to the fashionable neighborhood guys, (they didn't have day jobs, they were all in bands) from eight in the morning until three in the afternoon. Then, smelling of eggs and espresso, I jumped on the L train to Union Square to wait for it to be Luke's turn to go on lunch break. Too many hours of mine in New York City have been killed at Union Square, in the grass, eavesdropping and people-watching, while waiting to meet someone from the Strand for his or her lunch break. In Luke's case, a liquid lunch break.

In red Espadrilles and tight black shorts, I'd carefully chosen what to wear the first time we met up. "Hey, it's the little sister. I told everyone that I was going to meet an angel," Luke said, greeting me by the dollar book carts, smoking a skinny clove. The humidity was brutal, so he introduced me to the air-conditioned, happy-hour-all-day Bar None on Second Avenue. We talked about the Strand over three drinks each.

"I feel like Einstein selling hot dogs," he said, about his job shelving books in the psychology section.

"Basically a shitload of potential is going down the drain every day. And this is your life, you realize. It's vanishing minute by minute."

I was listening, eating up every word.

"The days are nearly robbed from you. Your time in New York is spent at work; and what are we left with? Maybe time to speak with a loved one? Jack off? Eat a fetus?" We drank cranberry juice and vodka until I had to walk him back to work.

Every Tuesday I'd wait for Luke to ring the bell after Trev left the apartment for the Strand. Timed impeccably, I'd dash down the stairs to find him sweating with his hair in a ponytail and trusty Tropicana bottle filled with high-alcohol-content vodka and a splash of cranberry juice under his arm.

I was always excited when he was wearing his back-pack—that's where the treasures were kept. Cassette tapes he'd recorded of himself singing to me: *When you smile, serious ideas get drowsy and my blood reddens. When you do nice things for me all heavy industry shuts down.* The tapes came with handmade paper covers where he'd drawn angels and graffiti that read, 'Chloe, get to know me.' A little baggie of dope that he'd pull out and flick with his middle finger while saying, "Let's cut the bullshit." Poems he'd written for me with lines like: *Small blonde locks fall on shoulders full of faith.*

Drinking and making love and doing dope until the sun went down, we'd listen to music and talk about people from the Strand. Towards twilight, we roamed the streets of Williamsburg, stroking one another's egos and bodies. "I adore you," was his favorite thing to say, and we'd walk to the waterfront.

I wasn't concerned about Luke's motives, though many people were pulling me aside at bars to warn me about him. I didn't care. I was simply enamored with him. To me, he was Jack-of-all-trades—a musician on a record label, an artist on a website, an exciting New York companion. I remember the first few times we slept together. I had to hold his long hair out of our faces, at the nape of his neck, something I'd never had to do before. *I've never been with someone so eccentric,* I'd think, mentally patting myself on the back. Sometimes, when no one was home and I was hungry for him, I'd put on "Art Floor Girls" and masturbate to it on the living room floor. In my head, I fantasized that the entire earth could see him singing—but that his eyes were solely for me.

August arrived. I showed up for work one morning to find the café shut down on zero notice except for a handwritten sign on the door from the owner. I dialed the Strand and asked for my brother while I walked down Bedford Avenue in tears. I wasn't looking forward to going back to the hellish New York City job-hunting. Just a month later though, I found a sales job at a jewelry store on the Upper West Side. Trevor was promoted from basement boy to a managerial position on the rare books floor of the Strand.

Summer ended and so did my relationship with Luke. Everyone is beautiful at first. But now it was autumn. The leaves crippled and died, reminding us that we, too, were only human.

"I'm not going to say that Luke doesn't feel something for you, because he does." Eric caught me outside of the bar Royal Oak, where I was taking a dance break and getting some air. I'd asked him where Luke was. "But what you need to understand is that Luke feels something for almost *everyone*. When I slept in a bed with him one night, he wanted to cuddle with *me*."

A lot of Eric's stories began that way: "When I slept in a bed with him/her one night...." My mom was deeply affected by Eric's tattoo of his mother on his arm, but she didn't know that his attitude towards the world was also tattooed on his body. "CHUG LIFE," his stomach declared in a giant black gothic font.

"That Eric," Luke used to say, shaking his head, "he's really something special." It was true. Eric chugged life, just like his tattoo ordered. If I *wasn't* up for meeting more of his off-beat friends from Amarillo, dancing at multiple bars, wrestling in the street, eating Trail's Best beef and cheese from bodegas, going to an *after* after-party, and then eventually unwinding at seven in the morning chainsmoking out of my kitchen window, trying to keep my heavy eyelids open, while Eric did line after line of coke showing me R. Kelly and George Bush YouTube videos—then I usually didn't answer my phone when he called. The bruises I woke up with the morning after weren't worth it.

Though we were no longer lovers when the leaves started to fall, Luke and I stayed friends. I would ditch whatever I was doing if he wanted to see me. I'd ride the L train out to Bushwick and walk the desolate streets to 703 Fairview Avenue, always liking the irony of his cookie-cutter street name clashing with his un-cookie-cutter self. "I thought you'd left New York," he'd whisper into my ear while holding me close at the bottom of his stairwell. On the floor in his cluttered bedroom, we'd make sculptures with candle wax, or a collage of vaginas. Once he taught me to melt down the heroin onto a spoon and snort the hot liquid on that bedroom floor. We listened to Smog or the Cocteau Twins and hugged each other to sleep.

But I'd wake up to him wailing. Luke had night terrors.

"I'm ugly and everyone at the Strand thinks I'm a faggot! Even *you* think I'm a faggot like everyone else!"

He held me too tight, shuddering and shivering, hurling his legs and fists at the wall, tangling the sheets.

"And I'm so scared," he'd cling to me and whimper, "My teeth hurt, my ass hurts, I've got a monkey on my back, I never say the right things. I'm cruel beyond my years. I'm cruel and alone and ready for obscurity." And with my head on his chest I could just about feel his spirit draining. It was like putting a baby to bed. He was so vulnerable that it seemed if I touched him in the wrong place or hugged him too hard, he might just crumble right there in my arms, and I'd be held liable. So I kept holding him—gently, because that was all I knew to do.

See, the problem was, I wasn't in love with Luke—I wanted to *be* Luke. Not the Luke whose demons emerged after midnight when we were alone, sweating in his twin bed. Not the Luke who blemished the blue sheets with tears, confessing to me he was frightened of being left alone. No. I wanted to be Luke when we were in public. I wanted to be Luke when he was zealous and cocky. He was the kind of person that wanted to sit on the floor and smoke pot and show you their baby pictures all night. The kind of person that tries on your roommate's green fur coat and kisses you on the fire escape and then sneaks into the bathroom to do heroin, and comes out and asks you to braid his hair. The kind that wanted to show you the Antony and the Johnsons lyrics that he had taped to his fridge. The kind that could turn on you at any moment. The kind that makes every following relationship look pale.

After I'd assure him, promise him, and *guarantee* him that no one at the Strand thought he was an ugly faggot, and that *I* didn't think he was an ugly faggot, his weeping would gradually lessen, and he would sleep.

Then I could relish in his surroundings, the aura of him that filled the room. I could smoke his cloves on my heroin high and saunter around his artistically charged room like it was a museum. The vibrancy gave me anxiety—I didn't want to overlook anything. The heaps of Polaroids, mounds of colorful shirts, piles of unfinished collages, milk crates exploding with art supplies, boxes brimming with trinkets, and steep stacks of rare edition books trimming the walls. I'd brush my hand over his Burroughs and Graham Greene novels, his Bukowski and Ginsberg poems. Sometimes I gave in to the temptation to steal. I made mental note of his records. I stared firmly at his family photos and touched his passionate acrylic paintings, trying to see into his brain and understand his soul. It was as though Luke had the secret knowledge of how to be fascinating, and I had this idea that if I just slept next to him, fondled his art and read his books, then maybe the secret would rub off on me, too. I sought to seep every inch of him into my veins.

I kind of wanted to be Sam, too. Everyone I met in those days seemed exceptionally exotic and exciting. It was Sam who informed me that the idea of seven dog years to one human year is an urban legend. "What it is," he patiently clarified, while alphabetizing the dollar carts in front of the Strand, "Is that one human year in *New York City* equals seven human years." I drank my coffee and thought about how true that seemed, while I admired Sam.

Sam is also the one who gave me a notebook when I began writing every day. I opened it recently and read the first page: "Sam gave me a journal, so everything will be okay."

The thing was, I never bought a book at the Strand. The Strand was never a bookstore to me. It was a venue. The place my brother and his friends worked. It was a place to check my bags before I went to apply for jobs. It was the place to pee when I was stuck in the city. The place to put on makeup before getting drinks with Luke. The Strand was my default location in New York if I wanted to feel part of something. There, everyone knew who I was.

Following the New Year, we had a staff meeting at the jewelry store. It was going out of business. I was unnerved. I took the elevator up to Trevor's office at the Strand, my throat tight and sore, and explained what happened. He convinced me to let him buy me a coffee at Dean and Deluca ("No, no, it's too expensive," I protested). We sipped our small, strong coffees while walking down 13th Street in the bitter January draft. He kept me calm, saying, "You'll be okay. You know, Clo, I think that as long as you live here, you'll be okay." Trevor doesn't know that his comment made me very afraid to leave—for panic that I wouldn't be okay anywhere except for New York.

"New York is the fast track to the hell train," Luke was saying one night. "There is so much here that there is nothing. Everything eats itself, nothing's durable. Trust fund baby nightmares. Broken-down rum-spitting bums. This is the hell of the world. Harsh callous tourists thinking it's all a goddamn Woody Allen movie. I'm sick of the trannies, gun-toting grannies, darting eyes and cock-sucking guys. I've fucked New York dry."

I tried to stay Luke's friend, but his I-hate-New-York spiel became tedious, particularly for someone like me, still a green New York devotee. Trev, Sam, and Eric more or less let go of him, worn by his moods. He holed up like a recluse in his apartment, drinking excessively, snorting dope, painting and writing. He showed up one night, annihilated at the bar Anytime, where I was with my friends. He interrupted us, talking badly about my brother and his other former friends from the Strand. "They don't get it. It's *just* the fucking *Strand*, there's *not* that much to do," he said, mocking their work ethics. "They abandoned me because I'm not a boring sober folk faggot," he grumbled. I left him there that night, unsure of how to handle him.

Trevor is a traveler. It's a part of his soul the way his hands are a part of his body. Like Luke, he was burning out from New York and getting sick of the Strand. He began planning his travel itinerary for the spring. Each night when I walked into the apartment, I'd find him sprawled out on the couch surrounded by maps, notebooks, atlases, and his laptop. "Clo, do you think I should fly or take a ferry when I leave Poland for Serbia, maybe stopping in Vienna on the way before the Guča Trumpet Festival?"

I was terrified for my brother to leave. He was the adhesive that held everything together. He handled the bills, he was my voice of reason, he was my connection to almost everyone I'd met in New York. He was the mutual, neutral one. Abnormally, I was dreading spring, willing winter to please prolong. Trevor's flight to Ireland was booked for the last day in April.

Luke cracked in February. "It's official," his email to me read. "I put in my notice yesterday. The Strand eats ass. They fired some kid in the basement for not taking out the trash. He forgot for fuck sake! I'm moving to Pittsburgh in about two weeks. So you should try and hang with me and help me pack. This move is gonna be so fucking great! I expect you to come visit me, because I will miss the hell outta you, my darling. Be careful. Be good."

I was happy that Luke was feeling alive again. That he was excited about life. But you come to New York as nothing, having to create your own mythology, and Luke had jumpstarted mine. I could barely digest my brother's plan to leave, and this wasn't a painless chaser. Luke moved to Pittsburgh a few weeks later.

Trev was right about me being okay. I seemed to easily fall into jobs, then into rhythms. I found work as a store manager for a jewelry designer's shop in Greenwich Village. I distracted myself with that for a while. I went to work early, took vitamins instead of drugs, wore dresses, tried to charm the customers the best I could. I'd come home to find Trev and Sam at the table, all set to work on some experiential art project or another. "Brooklyn Beautification," was the one in which we drew as many pictures as we could in twenty minutes and then covered construction sites on Bedford Avenue completely with them. Or we'd pass the typewriter around the table for hours, to create a collaborative story. Sometimes I'd just listen to Trevor and Sam have impassioned debates, such as "Pen vs. Pencil: which is the ideal writing utensil?"

"How's Pittsburgh?" I asked Luke, over the phone. "*Shits-burgh*," he said, "is really stifling. I was so drugged up and drunk in New York that I actually thought this place would be amazing. See that? Damn drugs. I should have stayed cynical, but nooooooooooo."

Luke came back to New York to visit for a weekend towards the end of March. I met him down the street from my apartment, at Anytime. We downed a few Cape Cods for old times' sake. "I should have never left New York," he admitted, his eyes looking up at me quickly, and then darting away even faster. "I should have known it was always just me."

It killed me to hear him acknowledge that. The rest of us had known it all along, mulling over what it was that Luke saw in Pittsburgh, knowing the whole time that he was just depressed. Pittsburgh couldn't fix it. I persuaded him to come to my apartment, to where Trevor and Sam were, confident that he'd feel better if he saw some old friends. He agreed, hesitantly.

We walked into my apartment, and Luke decided that he wanted to make a collaborative painting. Luke's paintings were always violent: skulls deteriorating, bleeding women, and heads flying off of bodies with the Manhattan skyline usually in the background. We sat on our knees in the candlelit living room with full glasses of red wine. We used acrylics, watercolors, and markers. I followed Luke's lead. The creation was a mass of emotion, a wash of red and yellow: blood and taxicabs. Elliott Smith was eerily singing, "Needle in the Hay" off in the distance of the speakers when Luke leaned over the canvas towards me, and kissed my forehead. His lips stayed there while he whispered, "I wish this was my life."

Great spirits emanated from everyone that night. Even the awkwardness between Luke and Trevor eased. I watched them sort of hug goodbye at the door.

"So great to see you, man. Make sure Chloe finishes that painting." Luke motioned towards me, where I was sitting Indian-style on the floor, sipping my wine and watching them. Trev gave him a discerning look, smiled, and said, "She won't." Luke nodded and smiled like he understood. I smiled then, because it was nice that they knew me. Trev closed the door behind Luke, sighed, looked at me and said, "He can be so cool sometimes."

I never finished the painting. But I hung it up over the fridge.

Spring persisted. Trevor's leaving weighed on me each morning when I woke up, every day heavier and closer to the end of April. Trev, Sam, and I went to Grand Ferry Park the night before he left. We skipped stones and drank a six-pack of Stella. "You're clocked out," Sam yelled after Trev flung his red *Trevor C.* Strand name tag into the East River. I eavesdropped on them while they said goodbye. "You're as good a friend as I've ever had," Sam said, before he turned his back up the hill. I watched my brother watch his first best friend's lean silhouette walk into the shadows of the trees. I linked my arm through his.

My fingers trembled typos on the typewriter keys and my foot jiggled nervously the next morning while I added Trev to my list of people that I love who've left New York. I didn't know how I would carry furniture home from the street without him, or whom I would pinch coins from in the morning when I was short for coffee. There would be no more notes on the kitchen table to read when I had an event in life such as, *"Happy first day of work in New York City, Clo!"* Or, *"Do you realize that this is the last weekend in your life, ever, that you can do something very special, very exclusive, underground, secretive, inhibited, and occasionally glamorous? Yes, that's right, after the next couple nights, you will never again be able to engage in—never again!—underage drinking!"* And,

"Clo, how do you feel about the fact that you are starting your new job on Groundhog Day? Think Punxsutawney Phil is going to determine your fate?"

I recruited Sam as my placeholder brother, until he told me that he, too, was leaving New York. He was going back to Colorado to go to school. Incredulous as to why anyone would want to leave this captivating city, and feeling betrayed as hell, I pressed Sam for three good reasons why he was leaving. He only gave me one: "Basically, I just like to keep moving."

Nausea slammed straight into my core the night Luke killed himself. I found out while sitting on the futon. I stared at the email that a friend of his had written, notifying me. I felt like I'd been kicked in the ribs.

It was May 8th, Luke's twenty-seventh birthday, the night he hung himself in his Pittsburgh apartment.

"What? No. What? No. What? No," I repeated while gravitating towards crevices and corners in my apartment. I tried to disregard the vibration of a text message he'd written me a little after midnight the night before: "All alone on my birthday. How cliché."

I lashed at the painting we'd made the last time I'd seen him. I wanted it out of my kitchen immediately. It was such a fixture of him, living above the fridge. I couldn't stand to see it and think of him every day.

I left the painting outside on the corner of Driggs Ave and North Sixth Street on my way to Anytime. I sat down on the bar stool I identified as his, the one all the way to the left. ("Closest to the liquor, farthest from the door," he'd once told me.) I ordered what he would have—vodka and cranberry juice. Still wanting to be him.

There'd been a time I was convinced anything difficult that New York launched my way was curable by coffee and a cigarette, by fast walking and loud music. The morning after Luke died, I exited the L train, equipped. My ears were headphoned, my mouth multi-tasking, taking harsh drags on my Marlboro red and gulps from my red-eye coffee and

I walked with tunnel vision as fast as I could. But the sting didn't settle. My eyes remained wet.

I rushed down Broadway towards the Strand, my head anticipating *something*. Did I expect a memorial for Luke? Was the Strand still standing without Luke and Trevor? I knew I wanted to see Sam or Eric, someone who'd known Luke with the same intensity as I. Hear someone say it out loud. It was the only place I could think to go.

However, Eric was not leaning against the Strand van chainsmoking because he locked the keys inside. Sam was not philosophizing while alphabetizing the dollar carts. And Luke was not going to walk out of the Strand to meet me with his backpack and headphones around his neck. I wouldn't hear his Discman blaring The Eels while he greeted me. He wouldn't sling his arm around my waist saying, "I've missed you, Poser," as we strolled down 12th Street to Bar None. He was not going to be around this corner, that corner, or perched on the cement wall reading *Interzone* and smoking a clove.

I just about choked on the stale thrift stench of aged books as I walked into the Strand like a zombie, my eyes downcast. I yearned to find Sam, but my safe haven basement gave off the vibes of a dark and dusty dungeon, and I became sick with the thought of walking down the stairs. Eric had once called it the "decrepit basement." That mourning morning, I couldn't have agreed more.

But I couldn't go upstairs either. Trevor would not be in his office on the rare book floor. He wouldn't be on the phone, or on the computer. His familiar eyes or smile would not acknowledge me through the glass as I plopped down on the chair to tell him my catastrophe of the month. He wouldn't tell me that I'd be okay. He was reading on a train to Estonia or writing in a café in Olomouc or thinking on a ferry to Helsinki or listening to music while walking around Copenhagen. Sharp, was the stab of Trevor's absence.

I was aware of how much the Strand floors creaked with each heavy step I made on my way out.

I stopped being able to get myself off to "Art Floor Girls." I tried, but it was daunting, masturbating to a dead person. Sometimes though, I would blast it so ear-splittingly loud while I took a shower that the thin apartment walls quivered. The water shielded me from knowing whether or not I was crying.

Bright red and yellow Strand shopping bags infest the city and Strand tote bags swarm the subway stations. I remain in New York, more than okay, and I wait for the day to come when those damn bags will fail to catch my eye—fully aware that as long as I live here, they never will.

THE PENIS GAME

Henri asks me, "Wouldn't it be…like…*so* funny if my penis could talk?"

He is three years old. I am twenty years older than that and I am babysitting him. I am secretly pretending he is my little brother. He is openly pretending I am Ariel from *The Little Mermaid*. Except he pronounces it: "Hariel."

In real life, we're cousins, it's winter, and we are sick of spending our nine-to-five together.

When I don't use my "Hariel" voice, (high-pitched and sing-song sweet) he gets huffy and says, "But remember? You're being Hariel."

In the span of two hours, Henri has changed his outfit from Batman to Spiderman to his "basketball clothes" to a motocross suit. All of these outfits include masks.

Now he wears nothing but the neon green motocross mask, declares himself "Naked Butt," and flicks his penis.

"Yeah. It would be really funny if your penis could talk," I answer in truth.

"And wouldn't it be, like, soooooooooo funny, if yooouuuuuuuuurr penis could talk tooooooooo?" he asks. He's drooling a little.

"I don't have a penis. I told you that."

He stares at Diego and Dora on the TV.

"Henri."

"I'm Spiderman *DUH.*"

Well how am I supposed to know that you are Spiderman when you are naked with a motocross mask on, I think in my head.

Out loud, I say, "Spiderman, look at me."

He looks.

"You know I don't have a penis, right?"

"But I am *pretending* you do!" he says. He is frustrated with me.

"Oh."

"I can pretend that if I want to." He sounds snotty.

"Of course you can." I sound condescending.

"Because I like to, so if I *like* to, I *can.*"

"That's fine."

So now I am a mermaid with a cock. Okay.

A few minutes later: "Hariel, sometimes my penis is big and sometimes it's small."

"Is that right."

"Yup. Um, Hariel?"

"Yeah?"

"Um, I have to go poop," he says, and runs to the bathroom.

Finally, I think to myself, lay my head back on a pillow, and pull my phone out of my pocket to text people. Just as I'm beginning to relax, he calls out from the bathroom: "HARIEL!"

"What?"

"Come 'ere! Quick! *Quick!*"

I walk to the bathroom lackadaisically.

He is standing in the bathroom, surrounded by the Frida Kahlo paintings and looking proudly into the toilet.

"Look at my poop! Doesn't my poop look like a penis?"

"Not really."

"Yes it *does.*"

"Kind of."

"IT DOES!"

"Okay. Fine. Relax. Wash your hands and wipe yourself."

"I won't relax ever."

I leave the bathroom. Take a deep breath.

Hen likes to wipe in the hallway. It's like he can't stand to be in the bathroom doing it alone. While he is wiping in the hallway, the toilet paper is still attached to the holder and dragging down the hall. He stares at me with his mouth open while he wipes.

It's weird because I do the same thing when I brush my teeth. I immediately leave the bathroom.

Later we watch *Frosty the Snowman.*

"Look at him, look at him," Henri nudges me. "Look at his penis."

"He doesn't have a penis. He's made of snow."

"Yeah he does. Look at that stick."

"That's his arm."

"It's his penis."

"No it's not. I'm going to the bathroom."

He follows me and stands outside the door. There is no lock on the door. He opens it as I am pulling my jeans up and flushing the toilet.

"Hariel, did you know that you don't have to wipe when you pee?"

"Girls do."

"That's funny. Girls don't have penises."

"Right."

I grow bored of being Hariel so I pretend I am Eric, her boyfriend, the prince with the dark, almost black hair. I do a deep voice and pretend I am looking for my girlfriend, Hariel. Hen loves this.

"Eric, look how tall I am—I grew in my sleep last night— Eric—look at my penis—it wiggles when I dance—Eric—I know how to play hockey!"

In the afternoon, we walk to the gym at the community center down the street. I shoot basketballs and Henri rides around on his scooter bike and the toy cars. He's yelling to me from across the gym, "Hey Eric! Watch this! Hey *ERIC*!"

I don't know if I am paranoid or what, but I notice a few of the moms' and dads' heads turn to check out the five-foot-three blonde girl shooting hoops, named Eric.

A baby of about a year is there, staring at Henri, following him around. When we leave and walk back uphill to his home, I say, "Hen, did you see that little boy watching you? He wants to be a big kid like you."

"Yeah, he wants to have a big penis like me!"

We go back to the house and make a train track on the rug and play with Thomas the Tank Engine. Henri's penis is so small that it can almost fit into the connecting part of the train tracks. He walks around (naked again) holding the train track in front of his penis, the track sticking out about seven or eight inches.

"That's a big woody," I say.

He takes his balls in his hand and squeezes. "This looks like a frog's mouth, doesn't it?"

"Um. Yeah."

At 5:00 P.M. I go home. I was supposed to have a date and I'd been pretty excited about it until he texted me: "I want you to worship my cock all night."

"And I want you to worship mine," I text back.

"But I just want you to want my cock."

"Well, I want you to want mine," I reply.

"I do," he texts back.

He is a twenty-nine-year-old three-year-old. I bail.

That night I sleep with one of those Guatemalan worry dolls under my pillow and I am sure to pick one wearing a skirt so I don't have to worry about whether or not it has a penis.

If Henri is obsessed with his genitalia at three years old, I can only wonder what he will be like in twenty years.

THAT WAS CALLED LOVE

199 North Sixth Street
Brooklyn, New York

I am walking down North Sixth Street towards Bedford Avenue with my brother at night. I have lived in Williamsburg for roughly six hours. I tell him I'm hungry. I tell him my stomach is empty. He tells me I live in New York. He tells me to get used to it.

My brother and I keep a typewriter in our bathroom, in front of the toilet on top of the radiator. In black Sharpie we have written: **Please Continue The Story.**

I sleep with my brother's friend from the Strand bookstore on the futon. He is suicidal and musical and has long hair and a nose ring and I fall a little bit in love with him.

My mother comes to visit. I am having a hangover from heroin. She comes into the café I work at on Grand Street. I am behind the counter. She sits at the counter. I have my hair in braids. There is no air conditioning. I am so hot and depressed and want to reach out for help. A few days later, I receive a letter from her about how much she loves me and I fall in love with her all over again.

I sleep with a French man who is a thief and I fall a little bit in love with him.

My brother is leaving for Europe and I am sitting in the bathroom writing him a letter on the typewriter and crying.

You, Lauren, move in the day he leaves.

It is morning. It is Brooklyn. You tell me if I am always in a rush then I should make my eggs in the microwave as opposed to the stove and you show me how. This is something so useful to me that I will use forever and this is why I love you. Your computer is playing Dr. Dre and Snoop Dogg and is resting on the garbage can.

We see something that we call *The Jam Box* at Urban Outfitters. It's a metallic gold cooler with an iPod connection, speakers, and a strap so it can be carried like a purse. It costs fifty dollars. We have a roommate meeting and it's unanimous that this is exactly what we need in our lives. Not to mention a great conversation piece. We split it. Twenty-five and twenty-five. For months we walk around listening to The Unicorns and Clap Your Hands Say Yeah.

We sell our clothes most nights on the corner of Bedford Avenue and North Sixth Street with a sign we painted that reads "Cheap Shit." One night I am drinking rum out of a Coca-Cola can and the cops come and walk me home and give me a ticket.

We decide to go to bed early one night and wake up at five A.M. to jump in the East River. We go through with it. Then we walk across the Williamsburg Bridge. We are sticky and we are laughing.

156 India Street
Brooklyn, New York

We move in the day after Halloween. We are never home at the same time. You paint half of the living room teal when I'm not home. I paint the other half while you're not. You paint half of the kitchen coral. I paint the other half.

We have a party and leave a bucket of black paint out for free use. Our teal walls now have black gothic-looking paint all over them.

We do not have a couch through the winter months. We do, however, have a black trunk that we found on the street. You write the words "DANCE TRUNK" on it in purple paint. I sit on it and stare at the scary gothic wall while waiting for you to get home from work. When you get home at ten thirty, we take turns singing Sinéad O'Connor's "Nothing Compares 2 U" to each other.

It's my birthday. We are loud. We go downstairs and across the street to the bodega by the G train. You are drunk and steal a forty of beer. The man behind the counter catches you. When we get back to our apartment there is a white piece of paper on the door that reads: "WTF? You have neighbors." You take a pen out of your purse and write: "Sorry! Neighbors have birthdays."

We are sleeping in the small messy bedroom we share. In my sleep I kick your bike that was leaning against the foot of my bed. It falls on you. You scream. You leave it there and keep sleeping.

I think I flush a hairbrush down the toilet but I am drunk so I can't be sure. Our toilet does not work for seven days. We live with a metal bowl on the toilet and piss into it and dump it down the bathtub or sink drain. One morning you shit in a bag in the living room.

You are sitting in a rolling desk chair. You are wearing a headdress. You are wearing a magenta silk short robe from Victoria's Secret over your clothes and I love you.

I start buying Zebra Cakes every time I am drunk, which is most nights. You like the ninety-nine cent Utz tortilla chips. We wake up hung over with wrappers littering our apartment.

I tell everyone at a party that brie cheese can actually get you high. Everyone makes fun of me but later, in private, you tell me that you know what I mean.

We host something that we call Breakfast Club on Wednesday mornings with our neighbor and we drink champagne and smoke joints and eat scrambled eggs before going to work.

It is snowing. We want a snow day. We both call out of work. We pretend that we are Devendra Banhart. We cut out pictures of him and put them on chains. We hang pictures of him from the ceiling. You decide you need more trinkets. We make jewelry out of our combined junk jewelry. We go to the Polish liquor store. We buy Beefeater gin. We have a circus and jump on our trampoline. We prank call people. We write and record songs. We take the subway into our jobs in Manhattan in the morning with headaches. I always dare you to get off the train at the wrong stop and walk to the wall and back, to see if you can make it before the subway takes off again. You always do it.

We did a lot of cocaine at Grassroots on St. Mark's Place and now at four in the morning we are waiting for the L train. I am wearing a black skirt and fishnet tights. You are standing too close to the subway tracks playing with your phone and you drop it in and the back comes off and the battery comes out. I jump down to get it. I see a rat. I stay down there with the pieces in my hands and hold my arms up and yell, "I've always wanted to do this!" before some guy helps me out. The train comes ten seconds later and everyone who saw what happened treats me like a hero.

You buy bikes for both of us from KMart with your tax return check. We keep them in the kitchen and see who can balance on them the longest because we're too afraid to ride them outside.

We have no groceries. I eat condensed cooking cheese soup and you catch me when you come home from work. You laugh for twenty minutes.

It's your turn to make breakfast.

It's my turn to make breakfast.

You're wearing my jeans.

I'm wearing your jeans.

I am writing.

You are painting.

We are reading Bukowski and Burroughs in our separate beds in the bedroom we share.

You give me a toy brontosaurus and say it reminds you of me and I don't know what you mean by that but I keep it on my windowsill for three years.

In the middle of the night you steal a Christmas tree from where they are selling them on the street so now we have a Christmas tree.

I sleep with a man from my memoir class and I fall a little bit in love with him because he tells me that I am Batman and you are Robin.

We are sitting next to each other cross-legged on the floor drinking Bloody Marys. We have just done our laundry. We are counting our underwear. I have thirty pairs and you have twenty-four. We have an awkward moment and then I quietly ask you what you have been doing for the past six days.

We are walking around the south side of Brooklyn. It is hot out. We are wearing headdresses and drinking Sparks with straws out of brown bags. The cops pull up. I tell the cop that I just got back from Berlin and in Berlin there are some neighborhoods where you actually get tickets if you are *not* drinking on the street. He believes me and waives the ticket.

We buy a mini keg of Heineken and keep it in our bedroom. We snort speedballs of OxyContin and cocaine. We are playing catch with a five-pound weight. I throw an accidental curveball and smash my computer.

2809 65th Street
Seattle, Washington

My friends in New York call me daily. All I do anymore in Seattle is talk outside on the stoop to my friends in New York. My roommates in Seattle ask me if I am doing cocaine. My roommates in Seattle ask me how many minutes I have on my phone. My friends in New York tell me they are exhausted. My friends in New York tell me that they are at bars and that they are exhausted. My friend in New York tells me she stole a few dollars out of the Habitat for Humanity box to get a coffee. My friend in New York tells me she forgot to steal toilet paper from the Film Forum. My friend in New York tells me he snuck into an Australian girl's purse and finished all of her cocaine. My friend in New York tells me he lost the journal that I gave him at the 79th Street Boat Basin and he walked up and down the Hudson River in the dark looking for it in trashcans. My friend in New York tells me she may or may not have had a threesome last night. My friend in New York tells me she is going to Dunkin' Donuts with a guy she met on the street that loves Leonard Cohen. My friend in New York tells me she is reading my writing to a guy on a roof in Bushwick while they listen to PJ Harvey. My friend in New York tells me she had sex with a guy last night and that he told her she was like an amusement park. My friend in New York tells me the warehouse party he went to last night was fun until he accidentally put his cigarette out in a girl's eye. My friend in New York tells me she is in a hot Chinese restaurant and thinks she just got her period and should she get the crab legs? My friend in New York tells me she is sitting in Tompkins Square Park, alone and restless, and that she should go home and do laundry but doesn't want to leave the Lower East Side until something magic happens. She says that there was an Asian dude playing Oasis songs, which was great, but not enough.

Last night I described New York to a rock climber in Seattle. "It sounds like, New York is for you, what the mountains are to me," he said, and I fell a little in love with him for saying that.

SINCERE SENSATION

Love. I don't know. But there was this French guy from Lyon once. Once there was this French guy from Lyon.

His name was Adrien and he lived with my brother and me for a month during a winter in Williamsburg, Brooklyn. We met him through Hospitality Club, a website where travelers can stay with other travelers for free. I didn't meet him upon arrival because I'd been out late and he was asleep when I got in.

I was accustomed to waking up and stepping over strangers in the apartment. My brother and I had been actively hosting travelers since the fall. But he was the one who organized it. I was just along for the ride. And I liked it. Liked the foreign objects left behind by travelers: Vegemite, chartreuse, AHOJ candy to drink with vodka. Liked the things they taught me: to mix sprite with beer, to wear my scarf a certain way, expressions in their language. Mostly though, I loved seeing New York's magic through their eyes. I was used to the bathroom being occupied, used to suitcases flung around the living room, used to waking up to a Mongolian, German, Spaniard, or Californian in the apartment.

When I walked into the kitchen that morning, Adrien was at the table in a red T-shirt. It was New Year's Eve. He was writing on an index card with such flourish and I was amused. He ended his sentence with a dramatic stab to the paper like he'd just finished the great American masterpiece and he looked up at me.

That night, my brother and I were having a New Year's Eve party, cramming close to one hundred people into our tiny railroad apartment. Close to midnight most people started leaving to go to bars. Adrien and I were somehow left behind and found ourselves walking together down North Sixth Street. We walked to the waterfront and we found an old grandfather clock and we kissed. We brought the grandfather clock home.

The night was long. At some point I tried to sleep but woke up because he was putting something under my pillow. Something he wrote on the typewriter:

you are so exciting
wake up
and go outside
to smoke

It seemed to be the most romantic thing to ever happen to me.

We went on the fire escape to smoke pot and then into the bathroom where he pushed me against the wall and kissed me. I wore a blue T-shirt from American Apparel. I was stealing clothes from there often, and that T-shirt was my current favorite. I straddled him on the toilet and he told me he loved my breasts. I never realized how beautiful mouths could be until him.

In the morning, he was up listening to jazz and rolling joints and cooking for everyone that had slept over. He was wearing a necklace made of wood that belonged to my mother. I sat down at the table. He was whistling. He was explaining something to me and put his arm around my shoulder in a joking, cliché, overacted sort of way, and then laughed and said, "You think I am very strange man?"

I laughed.

On my way out the door into the snow to the bodega, he slipped an index card in my trench coat, on which was scrawled:

Last night I touch a girl after midnight and she moaned of a god who I hope was me.

He would walk around my room, putting on my stuff and putting my stuff in his pockets. I didn't care. We were walking to brunch one morning and he held his arms out to show me. Gold rings, beaded bracelets, rubber bands, pins on his sleeves.

I ended up giving him that wooden necklace of my mother's even though I'd had to beg her to let me borrow it, even though it wasn't mine to give away, even though it had a lot of history and even though I loved it, because I am the type of person who will give anything to anyone I feel I could love.

When I wasn't around, Adrien would use our Polaroid camera to take pictures of himself and hide them around the apartment. I came home from work one night and went to the bathroom to pee, to find that the he had positioned a photo of himself wearing nothing but a bright orange scarf on the typewriter. On the bottom of the Polaroid he had written:

I like sex. With flowers, with painting. I have no definition of my sex feeling.

I'd never experienced that kind of laughter before. I almost died. I am still laughing.

because every time i see someone dulce
i take the person in my arms...rimes come with rhythms
at midnight I will come in your bed

And at midnight he came in my bed. And at midnight each night for the rest of January he came in my bed. My twin bed that my father made that took up the entire room because that's how small the room was. We fucked every night with just bookshelves separating us from my brother's room.

"You are the first blonde I've slept with," he told me some time in the night.

I didn't reciprocate, so he said, "Am I the first Frenchman you have slept with?"

Awkward laughter in the dark.

One morning we brought him to a store called Junk, which sold exactly what you'd think it would. Adrien came up to me and asked me if he thought it would be okay if he stole something. I said it would probably be fine. My brother walked up to us mid-conversation.

"I do not know how to say in English? But…I am a thief?" And he pulled out a psychedelic-patterned neon neck warmer from under his shirt.

One of my most romantic memories of living in New York City happened with Adrien. We went to see the movie *Manhattan*. I had never seen it. We got stoned and then stood in line for half an hour in the freezing cold. He fingered me and touched me and kissed me through the movie.

"There were two funnies," he said, "that only you and me laughed at."

I had noticed it too. There was a part where Woody Allen is breaking up with Mariel Hemmingway and blows on the harmonica out of the blue. Adrien and I both laughed loudly while the rest of the theatre was silent. The other part was when Woody is shaking someone's hand and he says to him, "It's been a pleasure and a sincere sensation."

I caught him shoving condoms into my underwear drawer one day. French condoms called Intimy. "For when you are in love," he said, and I told him that he sounded like my mom.

The morning he left, he wanted me to take him to Beacon's Closet, a huge and trendy used clothing store. He wanted to steal knee socks. We kissed goodbye on the corner and we hugged and then we shook hands and he told me I was a sincere sensation and we laughed. I walked him to the L train and then I called my mom and told her I'd found love.

I felt bleak for weeks afterward. I had my blue American Apparel T-shirt, still unwashed, still smelling of him, and slept with it against my bare skin most nights.

The last letter he sent to me read:

hey pussycat,
i write you today because it's a good day, so much sun,
a city to discover. i'm loving that.
yesterday i buy a new necklace, one from india
it is ok to steal nothing, i have values
if you could understand some things,
yes to be in love is scaring
but we always find possibilities
to look for some sincere feelings anyway
you are sincere sensation with smart character
i so enjoy your stupid sensibility
hope you cant understand
with the sun who go to dream
i hope you remember how to follow the birds
i stay at one more apartment in new york after yours, but
it was strange like the music of the doors, i don't go back
there again.
and me, i was dreaming this night, i was walking on a
forest, alone,
and find a little dead sheep i saw a tent, a bear was
sleeping inside
i just run very fast after that
i am with my dad today and I cant smoke weed in front of my
dad its a pity
when you come in france?
love
your fucked friend from lyon.

MY MOTHER WANTED TO BE BETTY BOOP

My mother wanted to be a dancer. In the living room when I was a kid we danced to "Stop in the Name of Love" by The Supremes and she had a glass of red wine in her hand and she twirled me round and round. Years later, when I was a teenager, a man came up to us at a wedding and asked if we were mother and daughter. "You dance with the same sensuality," he said.

My mother wanted me to be an artist so she bought me cray-pas and canvases and put a purple beret on my head. She told me about van Gogh and Picasso and we sat on the couch looking at Carl Larsson books.

My mother wanted to be Betty Boop. Betty Boop was independent. Betty Boop was sexy. Betty Boop really had her shit together, you know? She vacuumed a lot. She always had earrings on and lipstick.

My mother wanted her daughter to be sexually free, since she was not. I guess that's why she'd leave *The Joy of Sex* out for my male friends and me in high school to look at. And that is what we did during our high school weekends. We ate grapes and studied vaginas on Friday and Saturday nights. I guess that's why she'd give us condoms with happy faces on them and condoms on lollipop sticks when she would pick us up from the ice cream shop. I guess that's why my mother was the mother that told my friends they could talk to her about sex if they could not talk to their own mothers. But the last time I saw her, she told me I was *too* sexually free.

My mother wanted a daughter that looked like Scout from *To Kill a Mockingbird.* My mother expected a daughter that looked like Scout from *To Kill a Mockingbird.* That is who she and her sisters had looked like. She thought she'd have her own little Scout. That is what she knew and loved. But my mother got me. A mess. A mob. I popped out early and happy and loud with a maelstrom of thick curly blonde hair. Green eyes instead of brown. Thick hair instead of thin. Voluptuous instead of skinny. No chicken legs. Not one straight hair. Never a pixie cut. Breasts by the time I was thirteen. Everyone was always asking how I got that blonde hair and my parents always said the postman, a joke I did not understand for a very long time.

My mother wanted her hair to be curly. She told me that having me was like having a kid with an Afro. That it was like having a black kid. That she was expecting a little Scout and that she got a blonde bombshell. Her words, not mine. My mom and her four sisters all had straight brown haired pixie cuts. Their mother cut their hair with bowls over their heads in the basement. My mom had never dealt with my kind of hair and she did not know how to handle my hair as a child. I was never the girl to show up with cute French braids or neatly done pigtails. It didn't braid easily. It was too thick for ponytails. The most she would do was one barrette or a headband. Also, I just couldn't be bothered to sit still too long. Finally she just let it go free. But my mom loves my hair. She always asks me to try to make her hair curly. It never works.

My mother wanted dimples and would try to indent her cheek with her finger.

My mother wanted to be Bob Dylan and in the car when "Mr. Jones" by the Counting Crows came on the radio she turned it up and she threw her hand in the air and yelled along with the lyric: "I want to be Bob Dylan!" My mother wanted to be Lucinda Williams. My mother wanted to be Michelle Shocked.

My mother wanted to play the bodhrán but once she learned how she lost interest.

My mother wanted to be healthy so when she was eating Lay's potato chips or Rolos in the car she would give them to me to chuck in the backseat where she couldn't reach them anymore.

My mother wanted to be a Buddhist and sat on a pillow upstairs in her bedroom to meditate. My mother often took naps on the couch after work saying, "I'm not sleeping, I'm resting my eyes."

My mother says that if she wrote a memoir she would quote Leonard Cohen in the beginning: *There's a crack in everything. That's how the light gets in.*

My mother told me that when she was little she thought that babies were conceived when you lied down horizontally next to a boy. But then her sister informed her that no, no, she was wrong. French kissing was what made babies.

My mother told me that if you are falling in love with someone then they are probably falling in love with you. I think my mother was wrong.

My mother told me I was "high as a kite" one day after school, while I stood at the kitchen counter babbling about high school and eating Stoned Wheat Thins, and she asked me if I could "please not get so stoned after school."

Before I was born, my mother wanted to be a mother, and every morning while she drove to the preschool she worked at in her red Toyota she pretended she had a child with her. She would reach out and touch the leg of the invisible child and say, "Watcha want to do today, honey?"

My mother going to yoga class. My mother going to therapy. My mother going to figure drawing class.

My mother's books next to the toilet in the downstairs bathroom: *Uncertainty. Anger. When Things Fall Apart.* My mother's books on the coffee table: *Van Gogh. Bonnard.* My mother's books in the upstairs bathroom: *Feminism and Philosophy of Men. Motherhood: A Gift of Love. She's Come Undone.* Sometimes there were caterpillars on the toilet paper and there are always cobwebs in the shower. The spiders in the shower were her friends and she says to leave them because it is bad karma to kill them.

My mother: Doing downward dog on the floor. My mother in cat pose. My mother in spinal twist. My mother being a tree. My mother: Taking off her bra underneath her shirt when she came home from work, and saying that it was the best part of the day. My mother: Standing at the counter reading the newspaper and eating pretzel rods. My mother: Crouched in a rectangle of sun from the skylight painting her toenails mauve. My mother: Running around in my head like a cartoon.

MY HEART WAS STILL BEATING

There were days when I preferred the boys I babysat to the adult boys in my life. To be a babysitter is to be part actor, part therapist, part housekeeper, part friend, part playmate, part athlete, part mom, part dad, part chef, part chauffeur, part waiter, and part saint, which I am not.

Take Caleb—the seven-year-old compulsive pizza eater. "What do you want to do?" I asked him at the onset of our babysitting session.

"Read," he said.

"Read what," I asked.

"Stephen King," he said.

Sweet, I thought. His mom is an avid reader with a basement full of books. I read Nick Hornby and he read Stephen King in silence, and his cat was between us. A bowl of frozen peas rested on the ottoman. He loves those *NOW* CDs filled with the top-ten hits of the month so we were listening to Lady Gaga.

He lifted his round blue eyes, lowered his book, and broke the silence with: "Do you even know who Stephen King is?"

"…Yes," I said.

"Oh."

"Why?"

"You just don't seem like a person that would know who Stephen King is."

Are you kidding me? I wanted to strangle his little neck, but he was right. I mean, how many Stephen King books have I actually finished? Zero.

I'm used to it. I got it all the time:

"Do you collect Pokemon?" No.

"Do you know what Bionicles are?" No.

"Are you good at drawing robots?" Definitely not.

"Have you seen *Star Wars*?" No.

"Did you read the Harry Potter books?" Hell no.

"You don't know a lot of stuff."

"I know."

"Why?"

"Why what?"

"Why do you know?"

"Why do I know what?"

"Why do you know that you don't know a lot of stuff?"

"I'm very aware of my strengths and weaknesses."

"You're not very good at football."

Then Caleb asked me how many pieces of pizza I was going to eat, and I said one, and he said do you promise, and I said no, and he said can you please promise to only have one because I want to eat as much of it as I can.

So I ate one slice of pizza and he ate four and got a stomachache while we watched *School of Rock* on television. When the movie was over he asked me if I could draw him a peace sign poster. I said yes I could, if he would go to bed right afterward. We went upstairs and I hung the peace poster on his door and we crawled into the bunk beds—him on top and me on bottom. We read more, which was great, but he kept asking me what page I was on, how much have I read, and when I told him—he smirked. When I heard his breathing get heavy and steady I went downstairs to masturbate.

Let me be frank with you: I'm not the world's best nanny. I have not won any awards or ribbons at it. I go to the bathroom when I don't even have to go to the bathroom to kill time. I am distracted. I am sarcastic. I do not listen. I am uptight. I am selfish. I am tense. I text while I drive. I make promises I don't keep. My chocolate chip cookies are spongy. I am impatient. I over-explain. I am existential. I try to tell them nothing matters. I tell them about cremation. I once asked them where they wanted to be cremated. The toy store, they said. They wanted to be cremated at the toy store. I told them they can't do that. It has to be outside. The toy store parking lot, they decided.

But for some reason the kids liked me. I made them laugh. I have always been able to make boys laugh. I am blunt. I make jokes. I will get on the floor. I play along. I play tag. I buy them ice cream. I bring them gum. I try to remember their birthdays. I laugh a lot. I let them win. I let it slide when they say the words: crap, freaking, sexy.

Despite the competitive pizza eating and reading, Caleb and I did get along. He has long bleach-blonde hair and gets mistaken for a girl often. He's chubby from all the pizza and he plays soccer and football. He's constantly trying to make money. He's either selling lemonade or making bracelets. Or he'll have some master plan—like having a bake sale for Haiti but keeping most of the profits.

We were driving to the beach one morning with the windows open and listening to Carole King's "Where You Lead."

"Hey Chloe?"

"Yeah?"

"Last night I had a dream you died."

I glanced in the rear view mirror. He was staring out the window.

"You did?"

"Yeah. It was weird."

"Did you wake up sad?"

"I don't know. My heart was still beating."

"Well, that's good."

"Yeah. People don't die until they're really old, right?"

"Usually."

"Chloe?

"Yeah?"

"My mom has cancer."

"I heard. I am so sorry."

"I want the cancer to die. DIE, cancer DIE!"

"Me too, Caleb," I said, for lack of a better response. I felt inadequate.

He was quiet and I thought the conversation was over, but then he thoughtfully asked, "Do you think it would have been better for me to be a baby when she got cancer or now?"

My heart clenched.

"I think it would be hard either way. But maybe now; because you are smart and can understand it."

"I'm not that smart. Actually, yes I am."

Caleb's mom described her son as a bull in a china shop and said she couldn't believe I could get along with him. "My son loves you," she told me. "He said to me, 'Mom, I told Chloe something and she laughed so hard she put her hands on the table and threw her head back.'" I love him too. It's true that he was the most argumentative boy I had, but I'm okay with argumentative. It felt like hanging out with my own mom. He was also the oldest boy I took care of—he's eight—so he was the most helpful. I have been lost with him on highways for hours at a time, supposed to be taking him to the Museum of Flight, and he always figures how to get to I-5 South if we are on I-5 North before I can and for that, I am grateful.

I slept over at Caleb's house for three nights in a row one week. His parents went on their fifteenth anniversary getaway to a cabin in Canada. He woke up at six in the morning and came into the bedroom I was sleeping in and he asked if he could go watch TV. Yes, go, I told him. At six thirty he came back into my room and asked if he could have pizza for breakfast, and I wanted to say, yes, heat it up in the microwave, but instead I got up and made us cheese omelets and lemon tea with milk and sugar and he flipped back and forth between Scooby-Doo and the History Channel. Then I brought him to his Montessori school driving a green Jeep and I tried to imagine this as my life and I wanted to scream.

That night, after Caleb went to bed, I was walking back out to the living room to watch bad TV and I saw his lunch-box on the counter. I walked right by it, but I knew that I was working, and that I should empty it out, clean it and pack his new lunch. I didn't want to. Just the thought of it exhausted me. Bored me. But then for a second I pretended he were *my* son, and I got sort of excited. I think if he were, I would become obsessed with him. I would be like Anne Lamott, constantly writing about him (I feel sorry in advance for him). I would want him to experience love. I've always wanted a son. My mom used to laugh because I would go to her classroom where she worked and I preferred the boys to the girls. I have always preferred boys to girls. I opened his lunch and examined it. I saw that he did not eat his peanut butter sandwich and that he only had a few bites of his apple.

The next night, Caleb and I went out to dinner at a place called Hales and split the nachos. I told him I needed a beer. I don't usually get up at six thirty and I needed to take the edge off. This is why Caleb is great, he was like: "Oh, do you like hops? My dad drinks the Super Goose I.P.A. because it's really hoppy. You should get that."

And I did. God bless Caleb.

We both loved the same radio station, The Mountain, and as we cruised home through downtown Seattle, we were happy. "Jammin" came on and he said, "I know this song! Turn it up! I know this song! Do you?"

"Yep. It's Bob Marley, dude. Everyone knows this song."

"But do you even know where Bob Marley is from?"

"NO. WHERE?"

"Jamaica! He's from Jamaica, mon!"

We cracked up and I turned the music up and for once I did not get us lost.

Things were not always that easy. Babysitter is a vague word, an obscure job. I am starting to think it is as real as a job can get—taking care of another human being.

When I lived with Caleb for those three days, he had a soccer game I took him to. Afterwards, he was fooling around with his friends and the ball hit him in the face, hard and fast, crushing his nose cartilage, and he cried like a baby in my arms while his nose turned blue. Another time, his little brother was really sick and I was instructed over the phone by his mom to get a stool sample from him, which I did, and then I had to drive the two crying and arguing boys to the emergency room with a plastic container of shit in my hand. And once I forgot to pick Caleb up at school. Enough said. He was good-natured and readily forgave me and later I was not surprised when he was voted class humanitarian of the first grade. I hugged him tight and apologized one hundred times and he hugged me back but rolled his eyes and said, "You don't have to hug me, jeez."

Then there were the moms.

I loved the moms. The moms gave me whole-wheat rolls, mangoes, chicken, homemade Indian food, weights, jump ropes, toilet paper and cardio DVDs. One mom gave me $300 for a bike. One mom gave me an Ikea bed frame. The moms count calories and pawn junk food off on me. The moms come home drunk and can't find their checkbooks. One mom came home, lay down on the floor, and told me she was wasted. She asked me about myself. "You moved here from New York? You're so adaptable!" she said. "You've done more than I've done in my whole life! Do you blog about it?" The moms tell me they were in my position not too long ago. The moms told me that babysitting is the best birth control in the world. They told me they remember what it was like to have roommates. They told me I can borrow any of their Anne Lamott and Pema Chödrön books and stay at their houses when they are away and watch On Demand TV. The moms usually overpaid me. The moms had thousand-dollar laundry chutes.

"You get what you get and you don't get upset," one mom explained. "That's what you have to tell my kids."

It became my mantra. That and, "Don't turn a good thing into a bad thing."

Here's the thing about kids: they do not care if you have to go to the bathroom. They do not care if your head hurts. They do not care if you need to make a phone call, if you are starving, if you can't find your wallet or your keys or if you are hung over. They do not care if you are experiencing the worst menstrual cramps of your life. They do not care if you are speeding and there is a cop behind you. You must be there for them. They are not there to be there for you.

Like the time I was slicing an apple and the kids were in the other room and I cut my finger, getting red blood all over the apple and the counter and I yelled, "Shit, guys!"

Expecting help. A little compassion. A little direction to where the Band-Aids were. But no, they just laughed a little and ignored me.

It's hard for me to have my shit together for the kids all the time.

The other boy I babysat on a regular basis was an energetic brown haired boy named Bradley. The first time I met him I said, "Hi Bradley, it's nice to meet you."

"Hi," he said, "I just got my hair cut, and she did NOT do what I asked her to do, I'm going to sue her."

"Let me see."

He whipped his hat off and he looked like John Travolta.

"It's not that bad," I told him.

"I asked for bangs and she did *not* give me bangs."

"She just didn't style it right. You gotta mess it up a little."

"Mess it up? You're a maniac!" he told me.

We were playing *Star Wars* once and while crouched behind the couch, Nerf guns in hand, he looked at me and whispered, in earnest, "I'm a cancer survivor."

"You mean in the game?"

"No, in real life. I'm a cancer survivor."

Later, I spoke to his mom about it and she told me he was born with leukemia. Then she told me, "Bradley thinks you are more of a buddy then an authoritarian." She didn't sound happy about that.

Bradley and I were close. He was the only person to give me flowers for my birthday. He made me necklaces and gave me stones that he calls "gems." We danced around to his Alvin and the Chipmunks CD, made up a secret handshake, and rode our bikes into town to get smoothies and play at the water park. His favorite toys were these things called Bionicles (which I'm still confused about—I guess they are a form of a robot created by Lego). I admired his creative mind—he could make up interesting games of pretend all day. But in every game, he would "win" out of nowhere because he had an invisible gun, or I was standing in hot lava, or the ball was actually a bomb and it exploded while I was holding it. It's grating after a while. The boys always want to win. If I didn't let them win they'd get tears in their eyes: "It's not fair!"

One spring afternoon, Bradley told me he was in a force field and that it was impossible for me to "get him," no matter what I did. He said this with complete pride, mockery.

"Then what am I supposed to do?" I asked, standing by the fence. I felt helpless.

"Well you still gotta *try* to get me. But remember—you're part Godzilla, part zombie, and part baby."

"Okay."

"So *be* it."

"How?"

"Make grrrrr-ing noises and stuff."

"Okay."

I hated my job at that moment. It's easier with the younger ones. I can give them candy or a piece of gum and boom, they are high on life. But the seven-year-olds are intense and it takes more effort. It takes being good at acting part Godzilla, part zombie, and part baby.

Eventually the game ended, and I thought I did well: I made him laugh by growling and moaning and falling down and throwing rocks at the ground, walking with my arms out like a zombie and saying "goo-goo gah-gah."

After dinner we went outside to have a pogo stick competition. All kids are narcissists, which makes my job easier, because all I have to do to get them excited is tell them that I will make a video of them, or take a picture of them on my phone, and that kills time pretty well. I can't usually get more than three consecutive jumps on the pogo stick. He can get six.

"Can you make me a fruit and cheese plate?" he asked, in a good mood, because he won.

"Sure!"

Bradley and I sat on the couch and watched *Tom and Jerry* and ate cheddar cheese, apples, and clementines. He moved close to me so that half of his body was on top of mine and during the funny parts he looked at me to make sure I laughed.

The boys never want to brush their teeth. They all say the same thing: "Imagine if I brushed my butt with this! Dare me? Dare me!" (The girls I babysit have mechanical toothbrushes that play a tune every few seconds—reminding you to brush your front teeth, then the side teeth, then the back teeth. They like to explain their toothbrushes to me. Show them to me. Ask me what mine looks like. If it's electric. *It's not.* The disappointment is obvious.)

After he "brushed" his teeth, we went into his bedroom and he got all weird and self-conscious about his penis. He changed into his pajamas and I waited in the hall.

"Don't look!"

"I am not looking."

"Okay, fine, you can look."

"I am not looking."

To abide by his parents' rule, we have to read two books, one each. He read *If You Give a Pig a Pancake* and I had to read *Star Wars.* I hate *Star Wars* so much. I just don't understand it. There I said it. But that's what he always chooses and I get so bored reading it. As though I am not even hearing myself when I read. But my mind is not anywhere else either. Just going through the motions. It's weird.

My point is: I was so bored reading it, so I used the same tactic I do when I am bored reading anything. Just to entertain myself, I pretend I am on stage. So I started reading really theatrically, and he loved it. I mean he fell over himself laughing. But after I did that once, I had to do it every time. "Can you do it in that funny way?" he'd ask.

When I'd been babysitting Bradley for just under a year, we stopped getting along so well. It was a lot of my fault. I got depressed, distracted, disengaged, the way I have in other relationships. When he wanted to play something, I made excuses, and when I did play, I half-assed it.

"You're no fun anymore!"

It broke my heart.

One night at dinner he was acting particularly out of character—really rude and whiny.

"What is your problem lately?" I snapped from the sink.

"You have no idea how hard my life is!"

I walked over and pulled up a chair.

"What do you mean?"

"I have to clean up all the time. I have to vacuum after every meal. I have to buy my own Lego sets. You don't know what my mom is really like. If you lived with me, you would see what it's like when you're not here. My mom thinks I'm dumb. When I do some stuff, she doesn't love me."

"I think maybe you are sick of being home with your mom all the time. School is starting soon, and you'll have fun in second grade. I did."

"I hate school. I just want to stay home all day and play with Legos and watch TV."

I reminded him that he liked writing stories. He was always writing them in notebooks. I suggested he get a journal and write down his feelings about his mom in it, and he seemed satisfied with that

I felt horrible for the kid. That image of him so distraught with tears falling into his plate of cold chicken nuggets stuck with me for days. I couldn't believe how the relationship had changed and I remembered what it was like when I'd first started babysitting, the previous October. He liked me to lie with him until he could fall asleep.

"Can we talk?" he'd whisper, his head on my shoulder.

"For a minute," I'd say, and he'd go into long detailed play-by-plays of what he'd seen on *America's Funniest Home Videos*.

"What are you afraid of?" he asked me one night and then waited, listening.

The question hung for a minute, because I was trying to figure out how to be honest but also not scare him. All I could think of, though, were extremes.

I didn't want to tell him I am scared of a rapist or a murderer jumping out of an alley way and killing me each night, so I walk with my keys with one in between each finger and I feel safer that way, knowing I could punch them in the eye, though I don't ever want to have to. I didn't tell him that I'd just read *The Highly Sensitive Person in Love* and found out that I have a fear of engulfment. I didn't tell him I am scared of being poor forever. I didn't tell him that every day when I ride my bike I am sure I am going to get hit. I didn't tell him how afraid I am of my parents dying and how even though they are both relatively healthy, tears well to my eyes at the strangest of moments, while I am on the elliptical, making coffee, or walking to the post office, and I envision myself having to fly home to my father's funeral and it makes me want to crawl into a closet and bawl.

"Dogs," I decided to say, half whispering. "I'm a little bit afraid of dogs."

But he was off the subject already, propped up on his elbows saying, "Wouldn't it be cool if…" And he was talking about Legos in a language I'd never understand.

We lay there a little longer and his skinny leg was flung over my leg and as he was on his way to dreamland he mumbled, "You know what?"

"What?"

"I'm a little bit afraid of dogs too."

"Yeah?"

"Yeah. I really am."

When his breathing deepened, I gently pried his head off of my shoulder and tried to sneak out of the bed in one swift yet quiet motion. I picked up my shoes and tiptoed down the hall.

The next morning, I arrived for work at nine. Bradley answered the door, averted his eyes and said, "Hey man, what's up?" acting like nothing happened—like we didn't just lie together in a dark room telling one another our fears.

Just like a man would do.

A year later, I found myself telling Bradley I'd be moving back to New York.

"Why?"

"New York is where my family and friends are, and I miss them."

"Fine. But you lied. You said you would stay in Seattle for a long time."

I told him I was sorry if I said that and that sometimes things change. I told him we could write each other letters.

We walked home in silence. Bradley wanted to watch *Animal Planet*. The TV wasn't working and he went behind it and started messing with the wires.

"Can you get out from there, please? You could get electrocuted."

"Why do you always have to think of the worst possible thing that could happen?"

I smiled.

"Good point. I don't know. I guess because you are not my kid, and I don't want to tell your mom that you got electrocuted. Also, if you got electrocuted, I would die."

"No you wouldn't."

"Well, my life would be over in a lot of ways."

"Yeah. I'd miss me, too," he said, smiling.

At nine, I told Bradley it was time for bed.

"Can I write?" He asked. "I keep a secret diary now, like you told me to. It's so awesome. I have to write in it every night. I hide it from my mom. I keep it under the mattress on the bottom bunk."

I was touched, and told him of course he could write, that I used to hide my diary from my mom under my mattress too, and to call me if he needed me.

An hour later, he yelled for me.

I went in.

"Remember how I told you I wanted to stay home and play Legos and watch TV all day?"

His eyes were glazed over, the same way mine get when I'm inspired with ideas about writing.

"Yeah."

"I actually want to force my dad to make me a treehouse, and I want to write stories and comics in it all day."

"I think that sounds like a great idea. Listen, I'm not going to tell you to stop writing, but it's ten at night and your parents are going to be home soon. So when they're home shut off that light and pretend you're sleeping."

"I'm just going to write a few comics now."

"Okay."

"I might call you back up to show them to you, okay?"

"Okay."

But he didn't. And at close to midnight I walked upstairs to peek in his room. Fast asleep. I felt nervous as I lifted the bottom mattress up a little and reached for his black diary with a brass lock that was not locked. I opened it and giggled at pictures he'd drawn of robots and aliens. Then I saw this:

The zoo and acwaream

After scool one time I went with my babysiter to the zoo it had cracadils. And snaks too. Evin a fuyuw zebras too. Than we went to the acwareum too. Had sharks. I lauv sharks a lat. And a lat of fish. I thot this might be a good goodby preysent. Il miss having her because I had a lot of fun with her. I hope she has a nice day at Nuwuawrk.

I pulled my knees into my chest and started to cry. Then I tore the piece of paper from the diary, folded it in four, put it in my back jeans pocket and quietly walked downstairs to read and eat ice cream.

NIGHTBIRD

We were so intimate I could puke. –Raymond Carver

We made love in all kinds of light. Broad day in overgrown green grass. Four A.M. fornication during cobalt sky in the bed we called the tree house bed. Fluorescence of bar bathrooms. It was pitch black when we'd whisper I love you. You made love to me, you pounded me, you did everything, and you would say, "Look at you. Look at you."

Remember when I was homeless that one night and you rolled your eyes and asked me if I was going to make "I'm homeless" jokes all night and I said yes? That was the first time I went to your apartment in Manhattan. Mid-May. My apartment in Brooklyn was condemned. You lent me a T-shirt. The T-shirt was white with a screened picture of you on it as a two-year-old.

Did you forget how starving we were after having sex? That one time we went to San Loco at 4:00 A.M. for guaco tacos and you said you always wondered about the people that were at San Loco at 4:00 A.M. and I said well now we are those people?

It was so cold in New York. I was wearing my green trench coat that night and you told me to stop walking so fast ahead of you because it looked to other people like you were some stranger—following me, chasing me.

Weren't you?

Later you told me you actually liked walking behind me so you could think to yourself, *I am going home to fuck that small girl in that green trench coat.*

Remember when you were so stoned that you accidentally ate your turkey sandwich from the bodega with the saran wrap still on it?

How about when I was so stoned that I accidentally drove my mother's car up a bike path thinking it was a road, got the car stuck, and left it there? Remember how we had to go to court in the morning?

After smoking and sex you always craved something sweet. I remember how you walked around the apartment, slamming cabinet doors and yelling, "There are never any *motherfucking* cupcakes in this goddamn apartment!"

It killed me when you did that. I never wanted you to stop.

Sometimes we'd sit on the stoop and share a Trader Joe's chocolate bar—remember?

I haven't forgotten what your eyes looked like when we were drinking near your place in Alphabet City shortly after that. I haven't forgotten how my glass of whiskey shook in my hands when I admitted, "Well, I am a little bit in love with you and I don't know what to do about it." I haven't forgotten how my throat hurt from swallowing to hold back the tears in my eyes.

Do you remember telling me that you were a little bit in love with me, too, and that you also didn't know what to do about it? Your eyes had tears in them too.

I know you couldn't have forgotten about the Obama sex. We were on our first fuck of the evening on 207th Street in my new yellow room. The cheering from outside. Chilly fall evening. How the world felt at one. Like a truly good place, if only for a few minutes. Fresh paint on the walls. A new president. The bulk of the world was in front of their televisions but you were inside of me. Afterward, we bought forties and celebrated with people out on the street.

Remember what an excellent mood you'd be in when I was coming over? How you'd wait for me at the bottom of your apartment building with a huge smile and huge headphones on your ears and huge gin and tonic in your hand?

Life felt gargantuan.

Don't you remember? How excited we were for our nights together—the nights we called, "Show & Tell?" How we would rush to the couch with books/poems/writings/pictures to show and stories to tell? How many bottles of Bacardi Rum and Johnny Walker and Dewars and ice trays we must have went through?

And do you remember telling me that being with me fucked with your nervous system?

And do you remember how many blowjobs I gave you while I wore my Discman and listened to Animal Collective?

Did you forget that the reason I got these stupid red train tracks on my back was for you? How I said I wanted to give you something to look at while you fucked me from behind? How getting a tattoo on my back started as a joke but then I went and did it to surprise you?

What about that black and white plaid bra with the pink bow I had? Remember how you liked to pretend you were fucking "a gutter punk" when I wore that?

Remember when we had sex and I pretended you were James Frey? When you pretended I was a girl you took home from the mall? When we pretended we were in Portland? Puerto Rico? Not in love? Remember when we pretended I was a hitchhiker from Nevada and you picked me up on the side of the road and asked me if I liked fruit pies?

Remember that time I was trying to masturbate in bed and you were in the shower singing a Hootie and the Blowfish song and it was and hilarious and intimate and weird and I couldn't come, because you were singing Hootie and the Blowfish?

And that fall, when we made coffee late in the day and sat in the living room feeling romantic and we each chose one of our favorite love songs to play each other? I chose "The Art Teacher" by Rufus Wainwright. You chose "Man in the Shed" by Nick Drake.

And do you remember telling me that I was the one who gave you the courage to admit you weren't that domestic man living on Eleventh Street? And after you admitted that, do you remember that I was the one to help you cart your belongings over to Ninth Street?

Do you even remember how *hard* you had me laughing when we sat in your living room on Ninth Street, high, and you read our Gmail chats from when we first met out loud to your brother and me in a Southern accent?

I remember you laughing at me laughing, and you turned to your brother and said, "Can you believe I met this girl? I can't believe I met this girl! She is so compatible with me! Yet not at all." And that made me laugh even harder.

And remember how our safe word was "nightbird?" But then we realized that safe words are actually dumb, because how are you supposed to say them with a cock in your mouth?

And the time I was in bed as soon as we got home with a piece of bread and you jumped aggressively into bed and called me Oliver Twist? And we wrestled for the bread and I was very pissed that you called me Oliver Twist and you asked me why I derived pleasure from being so combative.

Do you at least remember how happy I made you? How much we laughed? How you told me I was the closest thing to the woman you would want to be, yourself?

How furious I made you? How much we yelled? How I sobbed once into your answering machine telling you that I loved you on the surface but not deep down? How one night you emailed me that I was even more unstable than you were and that you would mail me my stuff?

And the time you pulled me onto your orange couch and we were high and you had me go to the website:

www.findatherapist.com? And we laughed our heads off looking through the pictures of them.

Did you forget about the mornings we'd lie in bed and tell each other, "I appreciate you?" And do you agree that the mornings when we appreciated each other might have been better than the mornings we loved each other?

And do you remember those mornings? Like, do you *really* remember them? I would wake up early, and you told me I was like a dog. "Do you ever sleep," you asked me, "Or do you just lie there waiting for me to wake up and play with you?"

I usually lied there waiting for you to wake up and play with me.

And do you remember that when you did wake up you would come on my stomach and then trace it with that green marker? And then we would smoke again and then we would laugh and then we would fuck again and then we'd put music on, and we would always agree on the same music and you would say, "This is why I love you—because you show me all of this great music," and we'd hold each other and whisper about how lucky we were and discuss our neuroses and ex-lovers and depressions and dreams again.

And do you remember that in the letter you wrote me, you told me that perhaps your love for me confused me into thinking you didn't have any love leftover for anyone else? Did you forget that you were actually right on par with that?

You say that you love me but that you love a lot of people.

You say that you have a lot of love.

You say that my mind is like an elephant's. You say that my memory is so good, I should go on a game show and compete with a guy that can tell how many matches there are, if you dump a bucket of them onto the floor.

Did you forget how one of us would usually *cry* when we were together?

It's okay if you forgot. We were smoking a ton of weed.

THE TRANCE DANCE

The first week of working at "the New Age camp," as I referred to it, entailed lots of bonding exercises, standing in circles, and playing embarrassing getting-to-know-you improvisation and movement games. Most of these games included hackey-sacks. My co-counselors taught classes like Cloud Gazing and Magic Cards and Live Action Role Play and Acro-yoga and Hula-hooping and Make Your Own Moon Cycle Pad and Radical Menstruation. I taught creative writing and counted the days until I was leaving.

During the second week of camp, when the teens either felt very comfortable at camp or very homesick, we had something called Girls Weekend and Boys Weekend. The boys and girls were split up and didn't cross paths from Friday evening until Sunday afternoon. On the agenda was a matriarchal linear circle, a power shuffle, and a sweat lodge led by a man named Medicine Bear. But what kicked off the weekend was the most daunting of all: the trance dance.

The girls were anxious—on the first day while unpacking, I overheard a very intense girl named Hunter warn the rest of the cabin that "Everyone will cry during Girl's Weekend. Even the girls that don't think they will cry *will*. My sister told me." The girls had a choice: They could participate in the trance dance or they could go to the dining hall with some counselors to play board games. But they were heavily encouraged to try it out.

We, the counselors, were there to assist the girls in not bumping into one another and lead them back to the group if they started walking into the woods. We were there to calm them down if they started having a "breakthrough," the new age word for "panic attack." If they were feeling weird and wanted to be taken out they were told to raise their hands. The trance music was thumping through the PA system as though we were all at a rave on ecstasy instead of a summer camp. The girls wrote down their "intention" on a piece of small white paper and then threw their papers in the fire. They stood in a single file line. Lots of nervous giggling. The girls were doused with incense. They were blindfolded with red cloths. They were put in a large field. It was seven P.M.

We spaced the girls out so they could have their own room to move around. I had no idea what was going on or why. I felt like it had to be a joke. I imagined my fifteen-year-old self partaking in this and in a way felt jealous that I hadn't had the opportunity. "There will be mirrors everywhere," we were warned during orientation week, meaning, we would see ourselves in the teenagers. Looking at these brave girls, their developing breasts, their hunger for experience, I understood.

Nothing was happening and then it was. The music blared and the woman that was running the dance yelled into the microphone about how we were all trees. How tall could we grow? We were all birds. How high could we fly? How *big* could we be if we *really* tried? Her voice so jarring and obnoxious that me and the other counselors were making eyes at each other. She was the kind of person my dad would describe as a "Quaker Nazi."

Some girls stood still. Some girls walked around the field. Some girls tried to walk into the woods and we'd take their shoulders, turn them around and send them back to the group. Why were they walking? Were they really tripping out?

Some girls raised their hands. Some girls danced their asses off. Some girls sobbed. Some girls punched the air. Some girls laughed giddily. Some alternated dancing fast, crying, and laughing. Some cartwheeled. Some mumbled to themselves. Some spun like ballerinas.

I felt okay at first. Then I wanted to raise my hand and be taken out. The sun was setting. The guidance counselor who was there to oversee things came around and handed the counselors mini-flashlights. I felt profoundly self-conscious and scared and spooked and super, *super*, sober.

This lasted for half an hour. When a girl had an episode and cried on the grass, kicked her legs and yelled, a counselor named Lisa would go over to them and perform some sort of Reiki and shake a maraca over their body. She was taking it very seriously and was creeping me out. She put her finger to her lips and gave me a fierce look when I was whispering with my friend Veronica for a moment. I felt like everyone around me was on acid and I wasn't which is almost as creepy as being on acid alone.

Then the woman on the mic told them now was their chance. She told them to yell things out to themselves. Things they were insecure about. "Tell yourself anything you want!" she yelled. "You're safe here!"

It was quiet and then a booming voice. I knew that voice. That voice slept in the bunk bed above me. That voice asked me what time it was every morning. It was my British black girl's voice. Nadia.

"I love you!" she yelled boldly, not a trace of self-consciousness.

I felt a moment of shock and then promptly keeled over in tears.

The other girls yelled what she yelled. It was dark now. A breeze. Goosebumps on every inch of my body. Teen girl voices in different pitches filling up the field with *I love you*s. They were excited and emotional and they were breaking my heart in half.

"You're beautiful!" another girl yelled.

"That's right!" the woman on the mic egged them on. "You are beautiful! What else do you want to tell yourself? What do you want to OVERCOME?"

They poured.

"It doesn't matter what anyone thinks!"

"You're not fat!"

"You're good enough!"

"Your parents love you!"

"Be whatever you want to be!"

"Trust yourself!"

After each new sentence that was thrown into the summer night, the girls hooted and danced and laughed in this deep throated way. They parroted each other and supported each other and cried and screamed "YEAH!" and "WOOOO!" I've never seen anything like it in my life. A cover of "Somewhere Over the Rainbow" done on ukelele now played through the speakers.

When it was over, we sat in a circle on the stage called the Mothership. We went around the circle and each girl spoke about her experience. They mostly said the same thing: "At first I felt weird and self-conscious but by the end I felt stronger and remembered who I really am." One girl said that once a boy told her that she was the "short thing that people hate" and she finally shed that. Another girl said her sister died and she's still grieving. The girls were sitting touching each other, holding hands and arms around one another. Heads on shoulders. One of the last girls to speak, Sage, said, "Well, I'm not going to lie or agree. I thought it was bullshit and I feel exactly the same as I did before, so I hope you're all happy. I feel jealous that now you are all confident and I am not." Half of the circle gushed to her in one motion and collapsed over her saying, "Sage, we love you, I love you, we love you."

We were told by our manager to "keep it light in the bunks tonight." Other years, there had been episodes. You burden a teenage girl with all of that and don't expect episodes? When we got back to the cabin, I told my girls I was proud of them. That I was so proud of them. They looked at me shyly.

They were quieter than usual. Calm. Retainers in and lights out. We fell into our little beds, trance music still pulsing in my ears.

Breakfast was at eight thirty A.M. But the girls liked to get up at the crack of dawn to start primping. I'd forgotten just how vain and tender, how insecure and confident, fifteen-year-olds can be. I forgot how much they love their eyeliner. They used eyeliner constantly. And then they started using Sharpie as their eyeliner. They passed around a small Cover Girl mirror each morning and layered on foundation and eyeliner. Eventually I went to the dollar store and bought a mirror that was in shape of a sunflower, so we could be a bit more civilized. It also made the cabin feel more homey.

The morning after the trance dance, Nadia said, "Can we have a heart to heart, Chloe?"

"Of course," I said.

Nadia explained the situation. The situation was what it always is. A girl likes a boy. The boy likes the girl. But the boy has a girlfriend in California. So the question was this: If the boy tries to dance/kiss/hold hands with the girl, tonight at the dance, should the girl do it?

I got too deep and began to over-talk it, babbling about how in the grand scheme of things it really wouldn't matter—they might not even *remember* camp—until Nadia cut me off. Without a tinge of anger or annoyance, but just matter-of-factly, she said, "But it matters now."

But it matters now.

Well said. I didn't really have anything to say after that.

Then Nadia said, "But guys, guys, guys. Here's the question. Do you think it's possible to like more than one person at once?"

My heart. I swear my heart stopped.

GIRLFRIEND

You have a girlfriend now, but when we were eleven we sat next to each other in art class and you got in trouble for talking to me and when the teacher said your name, you motioned towards me and said, "She provoked me!" I didn't know what the word provoke meant at that time and I wanted to know and I knew I wanted you in my life.

You have a girlfriend now, but when we were twelve I was your girlfriend and we were both in the play *Once Upon a Mattress*. We pecked on the lips in the hallway by the gym while a circle of kids stood around us.

You have a girlfriend now, but when we were thirteen we slept head-to-feet on Friday nights in my bed under the pink and white striped comforter that I still sleep under and we read *Chicken Soup for the Teenage Soul* aloud to each other and sometimes I cried at the stories and you laughed at me.

You have a girlfriend now, but when we were fourteen you taught me how to smoke pot out of a seltzer can. We walked to the cement tunnels at the Spencertown playground and in the tunnels you told me that smoking and not talking about it was the best. You asked me why I always had to talk about everything and I didn't know how to answer you then, but now I do.

You have a girlfriend now, but when we were fifteen and my parents got separated you started sleeping over again and you let me wear your red and white baseball T-shirt that I loved to bed. In the morning, my dad dropped us off at my therapist's office and went grocery shopping. You read *Seventeen* magazine and waited for me in the waiting room.

You have a girlfriend now, but when we were sixteen you would check for blood on the back of my jeans. You would block me while I was at my locker getting a pad to put in my pocket.

You have a girlfriend now, but when we were seventeen we learned how to hold the steering wheel for each other so that the driver could take a hit on the chillum or bong or bowl.

You have a girlfriend now, but when we were eighteen and I came to your house we stood in the sun and watched one of your llamas give birth.

You have a girlfriend now, but when we were nineteen I went to visit you in Providence where you went to Johnson & Wales culinary school and I played beer pong in your basement with your roommates and threw up in the trash can and slept close to you in your bed and we smoked weed out of a vaporizer and ate falafel in the morning.

You have a girlfriend now, but when I turned twenty you bought me a lottery ticket and I won twenty dollars and we bought weed and we drove in your green truck on dirt roads and you told me you wanted to be so good with money but that you were actually so bad with money and I agreed and am still struggling with that fact now.

You have a girlfriend now, but when we were twenty-one you came to visit me in New York City. We met somewhere near Twelfth Street and saw each other from afar. It was like a movie moment and we ran to hug each other. You were drinking Gatorade and I asked you, "People still drink Gatorade?" We put my white comforter on the floor in the living room and called it a day bed and slept there listening to Okkervil River.

You have a girlfriend now, but you used to have a pig, Nelly Jewel, that blocked the front of the door to your house and you had parrots and cats and little black kids that your mother adopted with ludicrous names. You have a girlfriend now, but I have photos of us from all of my birthdays and you are next to me while I turned thirteen, fourteen, fifteen, sixteen, seventeen, eighteen, nineteen, twenty, twenty-one. You have a girlfriend now, but you used to text me your dreams in the morning and I used to sleep with my face in your armpit. You have a girlfriend now, but you used to make sure I ate, like when I was depressed, you'd say, "You have to eat something real," and when I'd order yogurt and granola you'd shake your head with disappointment and order Huevos Rancheros yourself. You have a girlfriend now, but you used to make grilled sandwiches with salami and vinegar and cheese and you'd make your own pita chips with herbs. You have a girlfriend now, but one morning at your mother's house, after your brother's wedding, we were eating bagels. I ate mine so fast that you wordlessly put your other half on my plate because you knew I was still hungry. You have your own catering business now and you live in Colorado.

You have a girlfriend that does this. You have a girlfriend that does that. You have a girlfriend that does everything. You have a girlfriend that does nothing.

YES TO CARROTS

I wanted Yes To Carrots lotion. I'd seen it in a magazine –
something like *Self* or *InStyle*. I liked how the packaging
looked, and I am not normally a sucker for packaging. The
bright orange capital letters and font were pleasing on my
eyes. And I love carrots. I love lotion. I love saying yes. I liked
the concept.

I didn't buy it though, because I didn't buy many things
like that when I lived in New York.

But you owned it. It sat on the back of your toilet, the
toilet you shared with him. I can remember a rush of surprise
that night when I saw it in the bathroom: *She has Yes To
Carrots lotion!* I had forgotten about it by then. I rubbed
it into my hands immediately, though somehow I don't
remember the experience—the smell of it, if it felt good,
or made my hands soft. It was the fact that *you* had it. You.
Had. It.

You.

I was a guest on your toilet. You are smart; you went to
Harvard, he tells me, and you probably assumed and maybe
even now know that I used that toilet, too. That I slept in
your bed. Put your lotion on my hands.

That I sucked your boyfriend's cock religiously.

No, really. I believed in it.

That lotion was one of the only things you had that I wanted. Of course, there were things you owned that I wouldn't have minded having: Your ass that's supposedly awesome, your book about how to be a good lover, your money, and your thongs.

But it was the Yes To Carrots lotion that I really liked. And the only tangible thing I saw that we had in common. Besides him.

A few months ago I bought a rip-off version, at Rite-Aid, I think. It had a similar look: a white tub with the words VITAMIN E in yellow and orange. I used it through the winter, and it was alright, but the whole time I wished it were Yes To Carrots, like eating frozen yogurt on a diet and wishing it was ice cream. I don't know why I didn't just buy the real one. Money, I guess. Or I wasn't ready for that image of you in my new apartment.

My images of you were the Polaroid of you on your fridge, and the large framed photo of you in matching blue shorts and bra on the wall above the couch.

The first time I went to your apartment, he fucked me from behind on the orange couch. At the same time, we both noticed that my face was about two inches away from the black and white photo of the two of you. He reached around me and flipped it face down.

We laughed. Genuine laughs. It was all still so new. It was humorous before it was hurtful. Naturally.

Your voice on the answering machine. Your side of the bed—*our* side of the bed.

Once I saw your bra—black and hanging over the canopy bed. I checked the size while he was in the bathroom. 32C. One size smaller back and one size bigger tits than me.

Fuck.

I looked through your things the mornings he left me alone in your tiny apartment. Smelled your perfume. Opened your drawers and perused your shelves and your closet. Pink disposable razors. Green flip-flops. Yeast infection cream. Receipts from Ann Taylor. Nordstrom. Eileen Fisher. Grown-up stores.

We (you and I) were ten years apart in age. Two days apart on your pillow.

I asked questions—of course I did. It was worse not knowing. I know you've been with girls. That you've been a dominatrix. That one guy wanted you to shit on his face, into his mouth, so you drank a lot of Dunkin' Donuts coffee ahead of time. Before that, you were a dancer. Sometimes I would masturbate to these things. When I watched porn, I'd imagine Tiffany Preston was you. Now you're an art historian, a professor, a doctor.

I've seen your naked body. He showed me a photo of the two of you once when he was stoned, his inhibitions low. It was black and white—headless. Your breasts are womanlier than mine. Larger nipples. Your pussy is well trimmed, small, like mine. I've seen the freckle on your thigh.

My obsession with you came in the healthiest of forms, because it lived without anxiety. Thoughts of him made me crazy. Thoughts of you made me calm. Your apartment was safe. You let me in.

On my bad days, sad and full of rage about being a side project, I'd Google your name: read about your thesis, your number crunching on patterns found in Mesopotamian women. I wanted to feel like I was in a dark movie about twisted love affairs, and I would go to one of your art history lectures in Boston. Watch you from afar. Approach you afterwards and tell you that I was your lover's lover. Of course, I didn't. The adrenaline would have been too much. Diarrhea all over the museum floor.

I want to know how you did it. How did you not stare out the window of the Greyhound with anger? How did you not kill me? Kill him?

And you made quiche, and you used Arnica, and I think you worked out, yeah, I think you did yoga.

But I smoked Bugler cigarettes in your bathroom (that you always tried to keep clean, he told me, you were high energy, he told me) out the window. One time he even smoked one with me, and he doesn't smoke cigarettes. I was sitting on the toilet; he was on my lap, my arms around him, we were drunk, of course. Your Yes To Carrots lotion behind us. Your cat the only witness.

And she's dead now.

I figured you had more important things on your mind—your dissertation and your ending relationship—but sometimes I was curious if you noticed how low the candy jar was getting. If you wondered why the stale Lifesavers and gum were suddenly gone. I almost cleaned the whole thing out.

See, I was always so hungry after he fucked me—hungry for eggs, for bacon, for bagels. But settled for Lifesavers and Winterfresh gum, because they were free.

I read a note you wrote to him once. It was in his sock drawer. Blue sharpie. Your handwriting is curvy, girly. We are handwriting opposites. You called him perfect lover man. *Perfect. Lover. Man.* It was such a nice note that you didn't think anyone else would read. It was only for you and him; and now for me. It was so sweet.

I will never be like you. I will always want to be.

The night your apartment caught on fire you were out of town in D.C. At one A.M. he came to sleep at my apartment on 207th street. In the morning, you called him. I heard how he said "Good morning" to you. He never spoke like that to me. It was sexy, like there was a secret between the two of you. It hurt my ears. The longer he stayed on the phone with you, the more weed I stole from him, the more muscle relaxer I blew, the more I contemplated jumping out my sixth floor window.

He was smiling when he came back into the bedroom. It was so sunny. I was sitting at my typewriter banging mean things on the keys.

"She wants you to know it's not weird," he said. "She is happy I had somewhere to go."

I didn't know which question to shoot first. I wanted to know how you are like this. How could you be so understanding? I'd kill him. Kill me. But my mouth felt cemented shut. And we had sex in the sun.

He used to read me things about you, you know. One time in bed, after you'd broken up and moved to different places he read me a piece about a summer day the two of you had. Tompkins Square Park. I told him it was too intimate, but he read it to me anyway.

Somewhere in the piece your favorite kind of bagel came up. Garlic, I'm pretty sure it was, with chive cream cheese.

You guys used to get bagels together on Sundays. Sliced tomatoes on the side.

I was never with him on Sundays. Mondays usually, Tuesdays sometimes; the occasional Thursday

Never Sundays.

A month or so after he read me that piece, I was blackout drunk on a bottle of rum wandering the West Village. I was crying; I was dancing; I was psycho, and on my way to the subway I went into a 24-hour Bagel Buffet and ordered your preferred bagel and cream cheese combination.

I wanted to see what it would be like to be your taste buds.

I didn't remember I'd done this until the morning when I had to backtrack to find out why my mouth tasted so fucking bad. The wax paper with excess cream cheese was still in my purse.

It was strange when you moved out: More dishes in the sink. Scattered beer bottles. Marks on the wall where your photo had been. He pointed it out to me, as if I hadn't noticed, saying, "See? The picture's gone," proving to me that he was telling the truth the whole time—that you were breaking up.

The bathroom was different, too: No lotion. No hairbrush. No age-rewind eye cream. It would be okay for me to leave a sweatshirt there now. Earrings.

Tonight I was at Bartell, which is West Coast for Duane Reade. They were having a sale on Yes To Carrots. I wanted to buy one of the products but I didn't know which and felt stressed about it. I wished I had read some reviews. Face moisturizer? Body lotion? I didn't want the same one you had. Some may call this objectophilia. Some may be right.

After dicking around in the store, I ended up buying Yes To Cucumbers eye gel. Then I was sad that I wasn't getting anything Yes To Carrots, so I got the Lip Butter, because it was the cheapest.

So far, the Lip Butter is great. I didn't need the reviews.

I bought it because I trust you. How could I not? We co-existed: one woman out the door, down the stairs, up the street, the other woman down the street, up the stairs, in the door.

It's been days, months, a few years now, that we've loved the same man. Of course I trust you.

I looked for you on the street. Sometimes I'd see girls in jeans, short kempt dark brown hair. There was a morning once, after leaving your apartment, that I remember a particular girl standing out. Green halter top. Sunglasses. My heart rate heightened. I know it wasn't you.

But maybe it was.

When we passed each other on Eleventh Street, *if* we passed each other on Eleventh Street, I was the one pounding your Lifesavers. I was disheveled and rushing to work with messy hair and faint bruises. I don't actually know what you were like. But we both had the same carrot-smelling hands.

ON SNOOPING

My lover and my mother both love Wilco, naps, Paul Auster, and *Six Feet Under*. They enjoy lying in bed late with the sun and drinking Trader Joe's Columbian coffee, listening to the birds outside, and reading. They prefer being outside to inside and they both painted their bedrooms a sage green. Last year they had to put their cats down and they both cried on the way home from the veterinarian.

As a child, I developed a way of life that some would consider a bad habit. I was ten years old the first time I was left home alone. The minute my mother pulled her green Saturn station wagon out of the driveway and beeped the horn three times—most likely on her way to either yoga or therapy—I unknowingly created a routine I would repeat for the next decade.

It was never thought out. I hadn't been planning it or secretly waiting for this moment. It felt natural. My body conquered my mind and I immediately walked up the stairs in my favorite colorful T-shirt that said SoHo NYC and soft plaid pajama pants to her bedroom and lay face down on her quilted bed to masturbate. Then I started with her drawers. I love my mother and even as a kid, I was painfully aware that no one would love me more than she. It was a confusing and reassuring feeling. I liked touching her stuff. My favorite item to fondle was her engagement ring: yellow gold with a bright green emerald set inside. I rummaged through her wooden boxes holding notes from my brother, my father, and myself. Pictures I'd drawn. Matchboxes. Sometimes I'd take a stone necklace or a peace sign pin to put on my backpack. I never thought material items could bring happiness, though I did wonder if the item had enough emotional value attached to it—it might—because it would at least remind me that I was loved.

Then the journals. There were stacks beside the bed. Stacks under the bed. On the nightstand. Sometimes under the pillow. Flowered covers. Plain covers. Matisse and Picasso covers. Lined paper and blank sketchbooks. I stayed there, on the bed, for hours, reading and retaining information and the dark and humiliating feelings of my mother that she, no doubt did not want her ten-year-old daughter to know of.

But I was addicted. The more uncomfortable truths I read, the closer I felt to my mom. The human condition fascinated me. Even back then I lived for words. As a teenager, I got even more into it. My mother taught me what mental health days were, and I milked them. Sometimes she'd take the day off too and we'd go to a museum or on a hike. But on the days I was alone, my day consisted of drinking Swiss Miss hot chocolate, smoking pot, napping, and reading the journals. It was my twisted source of comfort.

Did it cause me anguish? Yes. I recall the shock of finding out my mother was attracted to another man. The one time I went to therapy was after my parents separated. I was fifteen. I told the tall black woman that I'd read my mother's journal. I surprised myself by breaking into panicky sobs after she asked me, "And did reading it bother you?"

But. This was life. And I preferred hurt to ignorance. And it definitely hurt like a smack in the face to see my mother's annoyances with me and her hardships and unhappiness. But it also made me feel less alone. And I simply loved the words. I saw beauty in them. I saw beauty in truth. Truthful words moved me. Choked me up. I cried each time I read a new entry. In my gut I always knew I wanted to be a writer. But sometimes it takes people a long time to admit the truest things about themselves.

Then I turned twenty. And in June I moved to Brooklyn. There I found writing. And in my writing class—I found Dylan.

Dylan was the lover I'd always imagined I deserved. He was the higher thing I masturbated to as a young girl before I knew what I was masturbating to. We both grew up with mothers who loved us too much and now as adults we were obsessed with getting as much love as we could. We grew up on opposite sides of the river in upstate New York singing and prancing around our yards with dandelion crowns on our head and dirty heels. Our moms always wanted to be moms and Dylan and I spent most of our childhoods by their sides—our mothers who taught us compassion and that *everyone is equal* by buying us black baby dolls to play with. Our mothers, who listened to Joni Mitchell and constantly touched us and told us we were special and how much they loved us. Dylan's intensity matched mine. His morale matched mine. He was someone I could change with. Like with my mother—he saw *me*—the good, the bad, and the ugly. I knew this love was special.

I wanted to know why he loved me back. I wanted to know where he was hurting. I wanted to know why. I wanted to know all of the things he did not tell me in the bedroom after we'd had sex six times and whispered things to each other we'd never shared with anyone else. I wanted to hold his brain in my arms and hug and kiss and make love to it. I wanted more.

Dylan kept his journals on a shelf with his books. Black Moleskines, maroon spirals. But what Dylan had that intrigued me most was his collection of pages he wrote on the typewriter. He told me he did his most honest work on his typewriter. He wrote his rough drafts there so that he could not backspace or cross out. Hundreds of pages with that taunting black ink sat on a shelf attached to the wall by the desk. I slept at Dylan's once or twice a week back then. The nights were passionate and long with tears and multiple orgasms. Dylan left for work at eight in the morning. I didn't have to be at work until noon. I repeated history. I smoked weed, laid in that green bedroom with the cat, anxiety, hunger for words, my hand between my legs, and read. Sometimes I'd drink rum on ice leftover from the night before. I found some beautiful things. I found some horrible things. I cried and laughed and paced and threw things at the wall. I couldn't look away. As with my mother's journals, I re-read Dylan's writing for years, until eventually, I knew the words by heart:

Mother, 2006: I left my daughter today at her little apartment with her brother in Brooklyn. On the way home it rained hard and I got lost, pulled over, sobbing into the steering wheel, listening to NPR. Got home finally. House lonely without her, cried on couch.

Lover, 2008: Chloe lived in a crumbling mess on India Street in Brooklyn. The first time I went over there was a Monday or a Tuesday. I drove there after work during rush hour with printed out directions.

Mother, 2007: My girl's twenty-first birthday today. How thankful I am that she was born. What a love. Had yellow tulips delivered to her. "What a surprise!" she said tonight on the phone. Everyone should have flowers delivered at least once in their life. She sounds happy tonight. I knew her birthday would be. She did not need me there tonight. And that is a good thing. Her brother is good to her. Told me they went to the Art Bar and he bought her dinner and a martini. Then they got their palms read. She said the fortuneteller told her a man whose name started with M would come into her life. My kids laughing on the phone. I love them.

Lover, 2008: I met a girl in my writing class. She is twenty-one and likes my writing. A really great and compassionate person.

Mother, 2008: I am happy for my daughter, she met a guy in her writing class and I am glad she has someone to share her thoughts with.

Lover, 2008: As I write this, a twenty-two-year-old girl with blonde hair who may be a better writer than me is walking to my apartment.

Mother, 2008: I feel like I know nothing about my twenty-two-year-old girl.

Lover, 2008: She told me she loved me on the surface but that I am fucked up deep down.

Mother, 2006: The night before she left for Brooklyn she came upstairs and slept in my bed with me.

Lover, 2008: Chloe in Brooklyn. I don't know what to say about you yet.

Mother, 2006: This is what it's all about. Awake in the night to get a bottle of water in the kitchen and the answering machine blinking. I brought the phone to bed and kept it under my pillow in case my kids call. I must have slept through the call. Pressed new message. Rufus Wainwright, live, singing "Hallelujah." Tears in my eyes. What a sweet gift.

Lover, 2008: But God, the music you would play for me when we were naked on your futon. "Waterloo Sunset" by the Kinks is playing during this affair, except when we're fucking it's "Skinny Love" by Bon Iver.

Mother, 1992: I could be reading Henry Miller right now but instead I am at a meeting with forty women, waiting for it to start. Is this a waste of time? What is time?

Lover, 2009: Don't you understand, Chloe? It was like Henry Miller rang my apartment buzzer, came in, got drunk with me, told me he loved my writing and then made me fuck him the best I could. That's what you were like.

Mother, 1990: I have children that are afraid of me. I am the shittiest of mothers. My kids are shit these days. Run all over everyone. I scream and yell at Chloe then go into the dark bathroom and cry on the floor. Kids crazy, so much to do. Never sit down. Bake bake, bake. Hate being inside so much. Freezing weather. Quiet supper, kids in bed, should do that more. My son loved me as a three year old, now I never get a moment alone with him.

Lover, 2008: She has young skin. When we fuck, I look at her breasts and they make me harder and bigger. She has the perfect areoles around them. We met in a writing class, and besides an elderly gay man we were the only ones who bared our souls. Our stories were both full of drugs, sex, and a zest for life.

Mother, 1998: Yelled at Chloe, we slammed doors and I went on walk in the woods. Snow. Cried twice today in the bathroom. I am so tired and no one helps me. They don't know I am burning inside, I know I am lucky. Happy, noisy kids. I need to stop scaring the shit out of them. Now. Need to appreciate my day, my life, and my children. Tears are coming.

Lover, 2009: I'm preoccupied with the fact that I used to be happy and for the last couple of years I haven't been, not really, and I want to know why. I claw and I dig and I pay some old therapist in Croton to help me.

Mother, 2003: Had therapy tonight. I told her that I worry about my kids reading my down and out journals and thinking I've always been sad.

Lover, 2008: Amazing girlfriend, ugly lover, still not happy.

Mother, 2008: Brought Chloe's things to Washington Heights today. Reminded me of the movie, Pieces Of April. Only white girl on the street. I worry about her safety.

Lover, 2009: Some days I leave work early if I don't have anything to do and I go to her new apartment on 180th and St. Nicholas way up town. One hundred and sixty-nine blocks from my own apartment but I always go. White people are afraid of anything above 125th street. It's been hot as fuck and we drink rum on rocks and pretend we're in Puerto Rico like the book The Rum Diary and we drink and fuck and sweat.

Mother, 2009: Talked to her on the phone tonight, told her I met a man in a bookstore and he did a Bob Dylan impression for me. She told me she thinks people fall in love in the springtime.

Lover, 2009: Cried into the pillowcase last night. Why do painful experiences in one's life have to make me want to lie down forever. Haven't gone to work in a week. Walked her to the train and back home, chest buzzing. Called my brother except this time we switched roles and I was the anxious one.

Mother, 2001: How long would it take for them to find me laying down, dead on this rock. Crazy woman in America found in a State park. I feel the fear of two crazy men raping me. I wish I could swim, just take off my clothes and jump in, I won't though. I think my writing is juvenile but maybe if I keep going I can strike something.

Lover, 2008: I had sex with my first groupie. My first fan. I've never had one before. We met in a writing class in the West Village. At first there was no outward attraction. She was disheveled, kind of like the white trash girls I went to school with. On the first day she read a piece out loud about her name meaning green grass and how it became true because she was such a pothead. She always stood out to me.

Mother, 2007: I feel unwanted when I go to Brooklyn. My children walk three blocks ahead of me, they don't talk to me, and they ignore me and only want me there so I can pay for pizza. What the fuck? Not going there again. Maybe I learned something.

Lover, 2008: I fell in love with her. Not the bullshit love that is supposed to last forever with marriage and babies. But a pure and immediate love. She is a beautiful thing to happen to my life.

Mother, 2008: I miss my daughter, I love her.

I was never a careful person—I never put the journals exactly back the way they were found. I was too caught up in the moment for those details. I wasn't sneaky. "I always knew you were reading them," my mom tells me now.

I seem to be growing out of it. I see quite clearly now that it is a form of self-destruction—my own form of overeating, binge drinking, driving recklessly, or being in an abusive relationship. I understand that it is unhealthy for me. I can finally acknowledge that some things are better left unread. I can accept that people's hearts will break and so will mine. A small truth in all of this is that I've always wanted someone to invade my privacy. I guess that's another essay in itself— one that I am not sure I'm capable of writing yet. I am sorry,

Lover, and sorry, Mother, for ruining our trust and straining our relationships.

I can accept that all I've ever wanted is not very special—all I've ever wanted, like most people, is proof of love.

MASTURBATING WITH MOXIE

My mother and I are standing in the Atlantic Ocean with water up to our knees.

"Remember when I caught you masturbating, Chloe?"

"No! When?"

"When you were five."

"I wasn't *five*, Mom."

"Four."

"I wasn't four, Mom!"

"Yes. Yes, you were. You were on the couch in the living room on your stomach."

"And what did you say?"

"I said, 'I know that feels good Chloe, but it is something to do in the privacy of your own bedroom.'"

"And what did I say?"

"You said, 'Okay Mommy,' like the sweet obeying girl you were. Then you went to your bedroom. And you stayed in there for days."

We crack up.

She was joking about that last part, I presume.

Then I remembered. Mickey Mouse. I had this blue stuffed Mickey Mouse and it was plush and he had a bib on and I would mount it, and ride it.

My first fuck was Mickey Mouse.

At a Babar movie with my Nana in Albany. Six years old. She bought me Good & Plenty, my favorite candy. She took my hands out of my crotch when the movie was over. I wasn't finished. Hadn't come. Then we went to the bathroom and I peed and I will never forget her saying, "Let it drip."

Saved by the Bell on the couch after school. Kelly. Jessie. Lisa. Of course Kelly was my favorite. The romantic parts with Kelly and Zak turned me on. The parts where they would kiss and she'd be wearing those tight flowered eighties dresses and the audience would go: "Wooooooooo!" Later when Jessie did all those slutty movies, I was confused.

I am not sure if it was before or after the *Saved by the Bell* phase, but the first woman that turned me on was Daryl Hannah in the movie, *Splash*. I masturbated to that movie.

I was sixteen and listening solely to Tori Amos when I masturbated in a Virginia airport. I know. But I think she was the first person who had the intense words I wanted to hear. The intense words I wanted to write. My parents had just gotten separated and for some reason I think that had something to do with it. I would write her lyrics on my bedroom wall with a black sharpie. Later I found out that *Enjoy the Silence* was actually by the Depeche Mode. Made myself come against the wall in a bathroom stall to Tori Amos lyrics on my Discman while my father waited for me.

My bathroom floor in the house I grew up in. Light blue and white tiles on the floor. My mother would send me in there to wash my hands before dinner. Ages seven, twelve, seventeen. My face on the musty rug. My body liked the cold tiles.

My body still likes cold tiles. This explains why I like fucking in kitchens, in bathrooms.

It's like that question: Would you rather have sex in a dirty bathroom or a clean one? Someone asked me that once. I said dirty—no hesitation. Now I am thinking clean. I'm onto a different phase, maybe.

Masturbated at The Poet's House this past spring in New York City. Large windows. Sunshine. Over looked Rockefeller Park and the East River. Books. Words turn me on. White turns me on. Windows turn me on. I like masturbating in clean, white, wordy places.

Masturbated in an aisle seat on an airplane from the east coast to the west coast last Halloween. Blue blanket over my lap and my tape recorder with headphones in my ears. Listening to the orgy I participated in and tape-recorded two nights prior. A lot of funny and sexy remarks. A lot of moaning and orgasms. So turned on—couldn't help it. Thought about Brenda and Nate from *Six Feet Under*. Didn't they meet on an airplane and fuck in the bathroom?

Masturbated while writing this piece in the Seattle Library bathroom against the wall. Took me less than forty-five seconds. To come I had to lift my shirt up to feel the cold black stall wall against my tits.

Can't believe I have never masturbated in a car.

There's this little boy that lives next door. He is around six years old. He makes up games and battles and makes machine gun noises constantly. Today I was trying to masturbate and he was yelling, "All for one and one for all! I'm invincible!" and he made me lose my focus though he's pretty funny.

Funny thing is, have never owned or even used a dildo. I have never fingered myself. I like men's hands inside me. Not my own.

I've always masturbated to words. As a teenager, I masturbated to those fiction erotica stories on the last page of *Cosmopolitan* magazine. Really. As in: laying on my stomach, seeing the words that turn me on, coming, and lifting my head up with the article stuck on my cheek.

Also to music, I would coincide my climax with the climax of the songs. I had a boom box in my room with a blank tape in the tape player and I'd push the record button when a song came on the radio that I liked. I was an avid radio listener. I knew the words to all songs. I listened to the mainstream stations and Woodstock. So it was this mix of songs running into each other with no breaks—mostly the parts of the songs I liked—and I masturbated to it constantly. I got really good at either coming immediately, when the good part was coming up, or making myself wait for the good part. I think all this practice is why I can easily make myself come during sex. My masturbation tape.

I still masturbate constantly to songs.

I am starting to feel like a pervert at night. I have a ton of roommates so I have to use headphones while I watch porn. Because sometimes what gets me off is hearing the guys saying degrading things. So I turn the lights off, and the mouse is broken on my laptop, so I have this USB mouse and this mouse pad and they have to sit on the bed and rest on this David Sedaris book I never brought back to the library and I put on my headphones and search shit until I find whatever I am in the mood for. And there is range.

I won't say I look forward to that part of the day—but it definitely makes me giddy when I remember I can do it.

Things I have learned/acquired and things I think about masturbating: If you drink too many Manhattans at night you will feel absolutely horrible. Watching lesbians kiss helps your hangover. Lesbian scenes can make you come really fast if you just need something light and easy like that.

The worst things that can happen while masturbating: someone walks in on you, or, you are about to orgasm and someone calls or texts you. What a buzz kill.

You acquire habits from porn if you watch it enough. Like, I've been into wearing socks during sex. I must have seen it in a porn video recently. Any socks will do but colored ones are best, and not short ones—shorts that go up the calf a little. Thick ones. Knee socks, of course. Makes me feel younger. Tanner.

Europeans have the best videos. No question. At first I thought I wouldn't be into it, because I can't understand what they're saying. But it doesn't matter and you can insert what you want them to be saying in your mind. There's a German foursome I like, and two French couples I love.

A great way to have an explosive orgasm is to turn the sound down on the porn video, and put on a song that gets you off. Blast it while you watch your porn of choice. BAM!

Females are much better than males to talk to about porn. Males are over it. Done. They feel pathetic. I was talking to my friend and he told me porn makes him feel like a loser. I told him it empowers me. Males have been looking at porn so much longer than females. Females, on the other hand, have all kinds of things to say about it. At a bonfire a few months ago, I had a lengthy discussion with a girl about Spank Wire vs. YouPorn and both the guys we were with eventually walked away. Another guy said, "You guys know way more about porn that I ever will."

Porn is incredible. I sort of wish I knew that earlier. I did not discover porn until I was twenty-two. I was leaving a lover's house for work and wanted to hear the song that goes, "You make me come, you make me complete, you make me completely miserable" and when I typed in the link for YouTube, a clip from a website called YouPorn came up instead. It was a video of a girl giving a guy a handjob. I watched and masturbated and have been hooked ever since.

I like most of the categories. I like lesbians. I like strippers. I like socks. I like babysitters. I like The Milton Twins. I like lap dances. I like swingers. I like roommates. I like brothers. I like sisters. I like cheaters. I like fondling. I like wives. I like threesomes. I like foursomes. I like spring break. I like interviews. I like maids. I like punishment. I like small tits. I like blowjobs. I like kitchen sex. I like group sex. I like motel sex. I like bathroom sex. I like pool sex. I like massage sex.

And I like Mickey Mouse sex, because you never forget your first.

GETTING COMFORTABLE WITH BEING UNCOMFORTABLE (156 INDIA STREET)

Everyone who lives in Brooklyn is always trying to sneak the word Brooklyn into conversation. —Chelsea Martin

It was when our cokehead roommate decided to move out of the place on North Sixth Street, that Lauren, my best friend, and I decided we wanted a change, too. I was twenty-one and Lauren was nineteen. We'd been living in Williamsburg, in an apartment originally found by my brother, who'd since moved to Berlin. Lauren and I wanted something new. Something of our own. And we wanted that something to be in Greenpoint.

Lauren and I were falling in love. We were just on the verge of co-dependence. We impulsively jumped into the East River together. We smashed our phones on the street or dropped them into Margaritas and then said things like, "I just did that to make you laugh." We shared a Sim card. We laid on the futon and had *Flight of the Conchords* marathons, saying, "They're just like us!"

When one of us was down, the other made sure to be up. "We keep each other's egos warm in the winter," Lauren once joked as we walked home together, shadows and shoulders touching. We left each other "Have a good day" notes on the kitchen table. Whoever woke first would brew the coffee and choose the music, (either Animal Collective, Broken Social Scene, or Bon Iver). We chose each other over men. We chose each other over everything. We spoke in song lyrics. We slept in beds just a couple of feet away from each other. We walked at the same speed, we shared jeans and bras, and we read the same books. "You guys are like an alternative couple," one of my co-workers would often say. It was true. It was like we were dating without the sex.

Early on a Saturday morning in October, we stood outside of 156 India Street, in Greenpoint, with six other people, trying to keep warm in the crisp breeze. While waiting for the broker named Bart to come give us a tour of the apartment, we overheard one woman call her boyfriend and describe the place. "Baby, it's a complete shit-hole," she said, her face aghast, her eyes never leaving the building. She went on to describe the careless way 156 was painted onto the door, the front door's lack of lock, trash trimming the stairs and rats running around on the sidewalk. Lauren and I looked at each other and cracked up. We hadn't even gone inside yet but some people had already given up on the place. When we did go inside, a couple of people left immediately, mumbling "Thank you," their heads hanging low, losing hope on the apartment hunting game.

But we loved it. We found it to be hilarious. Sure it was a shit-hole. We wanted it. And we *needed* it. It was the only place we'd seen in our price range. It was $1200 per month. It was a one bedroom apartment. We would share the bedroom and pay $600 each. Lauren was working at the

Strand bookstore and I was the manager at a jewelry store in the West Village. We were both getting around nine dollars per hour. We got the "it's yours" phone call from Bart about a week later and we hugged and jumped up and down—delirious with joy. Our very own apartment. Lauren made a sign that read "God Bless This Mess." We moved in on the first of November. We moved in without shame.

India Street. We painted the living room teal and the kitchen coral. We hung bright blue Christmas lights and a disco ball. We hung Lauren's neon paintings. We hung a large square mirror by heavy chains. We hung up gauzy yellow and purple curtains. We borrowed heavy-duty expensive speakers from my father's music store and put them up in opposite corners. When I say we blasted music loud, I mean uncomfortably so. After we made the apartment look like disco fever, we had our version of a housewarming party. We left out a bucket of black paint for people to paint on the walls. We were sort of pretending we were Glasslands Gallery in Williamsburg. *It's experiential art!* we told people. *Paint whatever you want,* we said.

We had the rager of the year. The tiny apartment filled from wall to wall. People were climbing onto the counter and then onto the small refrigerator and jumping off. People were painting cocks on our walls. People were stripping and singing and at the end of the night people were probably having sex. After that, we were notable for having the apartment where you could go to act like a complete amateur. 156 India Street rolled off of people's tongues. "I heard about your party," they would say.

The repercussions of that party were rough. It was difficult to completely get the apartment back to normal, not that it ever was normal. We lived with ugly, almost to the point of scary, black graffiti on our teal walls through the coldest months of the year. We didn't have a couch. We had a table and we had a trunk and we had a mini trampoline. Most nights I would come home from work and sit at the table, half-heartedly reading *New York* magazine and trying not to get creeped out by the walls, while waiting for Lauren to get home from the Strand at 10:30 P.M.

Winter. We struggled with what many people living in shitty Brooklyn apartments do: No heat and no hot water. At the same time. That was the winter that we learned what 311 was, and we called it every single day, begging them to help us, to give us our heat back. Once I called and was so stoned and drunk I had a spectacular laughing fit and had to hand the phone over to Lauren. There was one night that we were drinking a bottle of Beefeater gin, (to keep ourselves warm, we justified) and jumping on our trampoline. At some point, I went to pee. I have a vague memory of knocking a hairbrush accidentally into the toilet at the same time I was flushing the toilet. For the next seven days, our toilet did not work in any form or fashion. We took the metal bowl we used for popcorn and set it on the toilet. Waking up in the middle of the night and pissing in a bowl in the cold, for seven days, does a number on the ego, no matter how you look at it. We went to the YMCA on Meserole Avenue and spent money on monthly memberships just so we would have somewhere to shower and shit. One morning, as I exited the stairs from the 1 train at Christopher Street, my phone vibrated in my pocket. A text from Lauren: "Dude. I just shit in a bag. In the living room." We constantly called the number we had for Bart, for he was all we knew of a landlord, and we left him messages every day about how we were cold and needed someone to come look at our toilet. Being ignored like that was shitty and hurtful, but we didn't know what to do. When our parents came to visit, we didn't want to tell them of our troubles, or how the front door didn't lock, so we would stand there, pretending to unlock it, our backs to them.

Regardless of the no heat and no toilet, we never really thought about moving out. We sent our rent off in a timely manner to Waterside Brokers. At some point that winter, we received a letter to stop sending our rent to Waterside. We were to make our rent out to a woman named Malina Nealis.

We complied without thinking much of it. We became comfortable with being uncomfortable. Come April, we finally found the motivation to re-paint the walls. The teal covered the black up, though you could still make out the painted words underneath.

On Saturday, May 17th, 2008, I left my job at the jewelry store and took the L train to the G train to Greenpoint Avenue. It was Saturday night and I was famished and needing to change my tampon. I remember feeling particularly burnt out that night—feeling homely, broke, exhausted.

I ran up the stairs from the G train station. I was glad to be going home, though I'd promised Lauren that I'd join her for at least one of two parties. There was one in Queens and one in Williamsburg. I wasn't up for either. What I really wanted to do was stay in and clean and write and get my shit together. But I didn't want to bail on her, so I planned on eating some oatmeal (I was punishing myself for all the liquor and red meat I'd been inhaling), maybe shower or at least change my clothes, and then call Lauren and meet up with her. And I needed to charge my cell phone.

I ducked under the yellow caution tape in front of my building, assuming it was for the construction work that my block was undertaking. I leaned my weight on the door to my apartment building to open it.

"Excuse me! Ma'am! You can't go in there."

I whipped around.

Violet fluorescent lights made me squint. A chubby cop got out of his car across the desolate street holding a flashlight. *Someone is dead. Oh my God, Lauren is dead.* My thoughts went wild and I pictured Lauren inside—drowning in the bathtub, hanging from a rope, or ablaze in flames.

"I'm sorry. You cannot go in there," he said again, calmly.

"I live here. What hell is going on?"

"The back wall of your building began to crumble and the third floor jutted out. The fire escape is falling off. One of the tenants called 911."

"Are you kidding me?"

"No."

The shock shaped a smile on my face. Obviously, our building was crappy—but a wall crumbled? A wall crumbled. Seriously?

"The Red Cross came and evacuated people to a shelter for the night if they had nowhere to go. Do you want me to take you there?"

"No," I said, I have lots of places I can go." It was somewhat true. The adrenaline was making me cocky.

He nodded, relieved, as if to say, "Conversation over."

"So," I began. "You're telling me that I have nowhere to live, and that I can't go inside, correct?"

"That's correct."

"Well, that's bullshit!"

I was yelling now.

"If you're telling me that I'm homeless and have to spend the night on the street, then I need to go inside and get my shit! I have to work tomorrow!"

"The electricity is off." He was so composed.

I motioned to his flashlight. "Can't I use that?"

He hesitated, then shrugged and said okay.

Leading the way up the eerie crooked stairway to the second floor, I didn't recognize my life.

My intimate and artistically charged apartment—now pitch black and dead—hurt my heart. The doorknob was hanging by a thread. The locks on the door looked like wild animals had spent all day gnawing on them. The alarm that I saw on the cop's face when we stepped in pleased me immensely for some reason. I looked at the apartment through his eyes.

Shit was everywhere. We had really, *really*, let the place go for the past few weeks. The living room was a mess. Scarves. Loose white paper with my writing. Studded belts. Tambourines. Small bottles of neon colored acrylic paints. Jackets. Mugs still halfway full of coffee and tea. Markers. CDs. Backpacks. Hats. Indian headresses. Suitcases. We'd gone to Seattle at the end of April and hadn't fully unpacked. Empty Jim Beam and Tanqueray bottles. Matchbooks.

Lighters. Journals. Books. Friends' books, my brother's books, my books, Lauren's books. A library handled by children. The futon was pulled out, bedded with Lauren's art supplies. She'd had the day off and was working on a painting when I'd left for work that morning. It was pulled out because sometimes when Lauren and I came home drunk from a party or bar, we liked to lie on it and listen to music. We'd usually fall asleep out there. That's what had happened a few nights earlier, and for no particular reason, Lauren continued to sleep on it for a few more nights. Kind of ironic, since the deteriorating wall and fire escape was parallel to her bed in the bedroom we shared.

The coral kitchen. Polaroid photographs of our life and friends lined the walls. They were held up by tape that had pictures of bacon on it. Dirty dishes were towered high in the porcelain sink. There was cold coffee still in the pot from the morning.

Then I remembered about my tampon. I looked up at the cop.

"Could I just have a few seconds alone in here?" This cop had a heart. He nodded, handed me the flashlight, and walked out.

I changed my tampon in the fluorescence of the flashlight, pretending I was camping, laughing in disbelief at my situation. I ditched my purse for Lauren's Jansport backpack. Then there was an overpowering feeling of responsibility of what to pack. The cop had said we could come back the next day to get our stuff out, but what if he was wrong? What if this was my only chance?

My first thoughts: Lauren's paintings? Books? My flash drive? Where the hell was it? Social Security cards? Where the hell were they? I opened the fridge. I was homeless now, for an unattainable amount of time—I'd need food. I saw the full carton of half and half I'd bought that very morning at C-Town. Surreal. My entire perspective altered. It felt like a movie set. Props. I'd been told this wasn't my home anymore.

I packed: Whole-wheat tortilla wraps. Baby carrots. One banana. One pair of Jeans and one pair of underwear. *The*

Days Run Away Like Wild Horses Over the Hills by Bukowski, a book I was planning on giving to a guy I was falling in love with, for his birthday. (Fascinating how my apartment was crumbling but I made sure to grab that book for him.) Journal. Pen. Phone charger. Lauren's navy blue zip-up sweatshirt with the red hearts printed all over it. That sweatshirt symbolized the beginning of New York City for me—I wore it every day the first month I moved to Brooklyn. Wallet. The latest copy I'd printed of the story I was working on about the Strand bookstore. Toothbrush. And that was it. I didn't even need my keys anymore.

I booked it down the crooked stairwell. I thanked the cop and left.

Totally exhilarated; I felt rebellious as I walked down Manhattan Avenue towards Williamsburg. I was speed-walking. I didn't know where I was going. I was so glad to be wearing my friend Lisa's black leather jacket and Lauren's black lace up to the knee Doc Marten boots. Both pieces made me feel tough. The perfect homeless attire. Underneath I had on a black button up dress with white flowers on it.

All the things that had been nagging me in my mind were now gone. Late rent, utility checks, dishes, laundry. I patted myself on the back for not paying rent on time. This was the first month we were late with sending in our check. And who gave a fuck about laundry when I didn't know where I'd be sleeping that night? It reminded me of that feeling when you wake up for school and find out that you have a snow day. All responsibilities for the day—gone. That's what this felt like—a snow day—but in life.

I uncharacteristically went into Starbucks down the street. I wanted a more glamorous place to charge my phone and break the news to people, like a bar or one of my favorite cafes in Williamsburg. But I was too impatient and excited to walk the twenty minutes to Bedford Avenue. My stomach was tense. To think I'd been hungry on the train just thirty minutes ago seemed insane. I had no cash. I went up to the counter and paid for a bottle of water with my debit card. I couldn't even drink it.

I plugged my phone charger into the wall. I really couldn't stop laughing. I called Lauren who was at a party. She left immediately and said she'd call me when she got off the G train. I called my mom. I called my dad.

One minute you're thinking how you are going to take a shower and the next you are in a Starbucks bathroom with a backpack wishing you remembered to bring a hairbrush. Lauren called me while I was still in the bathroom. I walked back to our "apartment" to meet her. She was talking to the cop. She was crying a little.

It started to rain while we walked down to Anytime, our regular bar in Williamsburg. The rain felt good. We stopped at Dunkin' Donuts for Lauren to pee.

When we got to the bar, we sat down at a table by the window. Marcos, our usual waiter walked over to us.

"Two whiskey sodas," I said.

"And two shots of Johnny Walker Black," Lauren added.

"Those shots are expensive," Marcos warned. He knew we only showed our faces during the happy hours when the well drinks were one dollar.

"Can you just get them for us?" I snapped after bantering back and forth about the price for a few minutes. I didn't care how expensive they were. I didn't have rent to pay, anyway. That meant I had an extra six hundred dollars. I could afford an eight-dollar shot. I was almost giddy with this whole adventure, and I couldn't stop talking. My excited babble must have gotten annoying.

"Dude? Is it going to be *okay* with you if I'm not *fucking stoked* right now?" Lauren interrupted and glared at me. I toned it down. She cheered up after the Johnny Walker Black hit her system. We downed them fast. "Let me see what you packed," she smirked.

We laughed at what I'd grabbed in a moment of panic. The heart sweatshirt, the Bukowski book, the baby carrots. It all seemed dumb but we ate the carrots and tortillas anyway.

We slept at our friend Chris's apartment on Eagle Street. He was a friend of Lauren's from the Strand. We woke up on an air mattress with a bottle of Tanqueray gin and Poland

Springs water in between us. Books outlined me. Ceiling to floor. It was beautiful. Where was I? Was I in a library? Straight ahead the sun hit the bright yellow Strand bags in the kitchen. Lauren was to my left. Ah, I remembered. We were at Chris's apartment. A book junkie's place.

Lauren woke up. She lay there for a minute, taking in all the books too.

"This must be what it feels like to sleep in an aisle of the Strand, huh?" I said.

"Oh man....yeah. He really does have a book collecting sickness you know."

We wrote a thank-you note to Chris for letting us stay. I went into the bathroom and was relieved to find Excedrin. I popped three.

It was a little after seven A.M. and sunny, when we dragged up the hill in silence to India Street. To the yellow tape. The cop car. The cop told us we had exactly one hour to get out. Now that it was daylight I could see that the yellow tape actually did not read CAUTION, it read FIRE LINE DO NOT CROSS. A piece of paper on the door read:

HAZARDOUS: FAILURE TO MAINTAIN EXTE-RIOR BUILDING WALL. DEFECT IS: REAR WALL IS ROTTED, DEFECTIVE AND PULLING AWAY FROM WOOD FRAME. FIRE ESCAPE IS IN DANGER DUE TO AFFECTED REAR WALL AND COULD DISLODGE IF USED.

And:

FAILURE TO MAINTAIN BLDG. NOTED: AT CELLAR OF FRONT BLDG=NO FIREPROOF ENCLOSURE FOR BOILER RM,MISSING FIREPROOFING AT CEILING AT VARIOUS LOCATION,ROTTED JOISTS NEXT TO BOILER RM, LARGE AMOUNT OF DEBRIS THRU-OUT

We began packing. We had no electricity, so we were listening to Elliott Smith on Lauren's computer battery just waiting for it to die. We could barely hear it. We dropped our laundry off at the laundromat. Then we reclined on our backs on the futon and waited for my Dad and Lauren's family. They were driving from upstate to fill their cars up with the stuff we wanted to keep. When the Elliott Smith music died—no pun intended—everything got too depressing and weird and quiet so we went outside to shoot the shit with the cop. We sat out on the stoop with our brand new bikes. Lauren had tripped on acid a few days prior, and while tripping had a revelation that friends were more important than money. Then she surprised me by buying us both bikes at K-mart. We'd ridden them once.

My dad pulled up shortly afterwards. We went to the back of the building to look at the crumbling wall. He took some photographs. Lauren's parents, sister, and brother, arrived. The six of us took treks up and down the stairs. Lauren's five-year-old brother was scared shitless and confused.

"Hey Chloe, Hey Lauren, is it gonna fall on me now?" he asked, while cautiously facing his fear and going inside. His arms were above his head with his elbows out for protection. My dad kept making me go back in to double, triple, quadruple check if I'd left anything important. The whole experience so jarring that I just wanted to get the hell out of there. I left my bed. My dressers. Clothes. Food. Kitchen utensils. Knick-knacks. Left it all in there to die, deteriorate, whatever. We wrote a huge *Fuck You Melina Nealis* to our non-existent landlord on the wall in bright orange paint. And we were off.

Lauren and I lost each other that next week. We had different work hours and we stayed at different places—me with a guy I'd started seeing and she with people from the Strand. The week was a blur of tears and other people's shampoos. By the end of it, I was lucky enough to move in with a friend for the summer in Washington Heights. Lauren moved to Bushwick.

But we couldn't let go. I don't think we exactly had post-traumatic stress from what went down at 156, but it messed our heads up pretty well for a while. We just could not get over it. We mourned it. We inserted the number 156 into everything we could. We inserted the words "One five six— you've got the dreamer's disease," into the song "You Get What You Give" by The New Radicals. We bought mailbox stickers and stuck 156 on our computers and cars. We looked for the number everywhere—were plagued by it. Once Lauren purposely got her bank account low enough so that she had exactly one dollar and fifty-six cents. Or we'd be at a bodega and would try to buy the exact amount of candy that would bring the total to $1.56. We were this close to getting it tattooed on our fingers. (We got worse tattoos instead.) One fifty-six gave us *baggage*. We couldn't meet anyone without launching into the story. We were craving closure.

One year later, we were drinking jumbo Styrofoam cups of beer at Turkey's Nest and playing Big Buck Hunter when we decided we wanted to walk to India Street and break in. It was like going back to an ex's house—you know it's pathetic and that you should be over it by now, but you aren't, and the brain says one thing but the heart says another. We walked fast, excited, and driven by nostalgia.

The building was exactly how we'd left it, except even trashier. It was boarded up but we were able to squeeze through a hole in the fence next door. Once off the sidewalk and on the other side of the fence, we saw there was a ladder propped against the other fence we would have had to climb to get to the back of 156. We climbed the ladder, and from the top, noticed a mattress in the backyard of 156. We were not the first ones to have done this. We jumped. The back door to 156 was wide open. We ran up the stairs, using our cell phones for lights. The door to our apartment was gone. We went in. The fridge was in the middle of the living room. Some of our underwear and old credit cards and photographs, still on the floor. A small shelf we loved that we'd painted neon yellow sat on the counter. We filled our backpacks up with our stuff that we didn't really need: thongs and Polaroids and the shelf. We heard some movement and the saw some raccoon-esque animal run down stairs. Lauren thought she made out the figure of a sleeping person in the corner. We figured people squatted there now. We became frightened and ran out. We ran to Lulu's Bar on Franklin Avenue. We laughed and spread out our "new" things on the benches.

156 India Street gave me anxiety to the point that for the next two years I didn't go anywhere without a backpack holding an extra pair of underwear and a piece of fruit. You never know. I've yet to be in Brooklyn and not walk over to 156 India Street to see what's going on with it, or to sit on the stoop and reminisce. Each time, it looks worse than the time before. A few weeks ago I Googled my old address. A competition on the website *New York Shitty* popped up. The website was holding a contest for "disgruntled Brooklyn renters." Whoever made the best and funniest thirty-second video explaining their situation would win $1,999. "I would strongly advise anyone who resided at 156 India Street, to enter this contest," the last line read. Alas, Lauren and I had missed the deadline.

YOU HAD ME

You had me when I was a teenager, so you got my best body, depending on how you look at it, though I was less comfortable in it then, than I am now. I had small tits that I thought were big, small hips that I thought were big, and legs that I thought were fat but were not. You had me when I was dyeing my hair super blonde from the box and had clear skin. I was so afraid to have sex for the pain factor so I clenched and clenched and clenched and you were patient with me for months and months and months until finally you whispered, "relax," and I listened to you.

And you had me close to this time because I started dating you while I was still messing around on High Street with the above mentioned. You had me when you lived on Main Street. You had me live there. You had me fill up a drawer. You pretty much made me. You had me when I was driving to community college at seven every morning. You had me when snorting narcotics was my after-school program. You had me when I thought I wanted to be a substance abuse counselor, not even noticing the irony. You had me when I drank Budweiser and loved the Yeah Yeah Yeahs. You had me when I was addicted to pills but also to working out. You had me when I would take a bunch of Aderall and then go to Kickboxing classes, getting my heart rate high as the sky.

And you had me when I was pathetic but didn't know that. Meaning *I* didn't know that and *you* didn't know that. You had me when I was sad and skinny and wearing clothes too big for me. A men's white T-shirt, jeans that were falling off my waist, a coat with a wool hood even though it was spring. You had me at my thinnest. You had me when I was scratching my face off. You had me when I stopped eating food (one Hot Pocket a day) and only ingested pills though I didn't chew them then like I do now. I snorted them, only.

And you had me at my prime. My easiest, my happiest, when I was light and dark at the same time. You had me in Williamsburg, in Brooklyn, in the summer. You had me when I was young and I knew it. You had me as a joyous, pacing, unemployed blonde girl saying please, please, *please*. You had me when I was vulnerable with excitement. You had me when I was at the point where I would do anything that I shouldn't do. You had me when I needed to party more than I needed to sleep. You had me when I was fearless in my ignorance. You had me after I'd learned how to make myself come. You had me when I had the ability to fall in love with any boy who lived in Brooklyn and read books and looked at me. You had me when I was so enthralled with New York City that I was falling asleep with gum in my mouth and markers bleeding all over my bed. You had me before I knew I was a writer but I read you some journal entries once when you were high and you told me they were beautiful. You had me before you died.

And you had me when I was confused and cold and adjusting to my first winter in New York. I didn't really know where my life was going and you made me laugh. You had me when I had put on winter weight and was somewhat depressed about that. You had me when I listened to Of Montreal a lot.

And you had me when I was finding writing. You had me when I shared a bedroom with my best friend that had an Aladdin poster in it. You had me when I hadn't had sex in almost one year. You had me when I was binge drinking with my friends. You had me when I didn't take my writing seriously and you took me aside at the bar and said, "You just have to take your writing more seriously." You had me when I was coming of age, I would tell you. Stop blaming your hormones, you'd say. You had me when we were touching every part of our bodies together and I would whisper in your ear, "I want you," and you would sometimes smile at that and other times look serious and you would always respond, "You have me."

And you had me when I was trying, trying, trying, more than I knew. I was trying to live on the west side of the United States of America, even though I didn't know what I was doing there and I hated it to an extent. I tried, mom. I tried to be Betty Boop. You had me when I would go to swing dancing classes and eat Valiums and Banana Nut Cheerios and you had me when I was a full-fledged nanny. You had me when I fell into a depression, when the only place I liked to go was a coffee shop and the doctor's. You had me when I stopped answering the phone.

And you had me when I was heartbroken enough that I couldn't even see. When I was waitressing and crying all the time, so much so that my boss said, "Give me your hand. Give me your hand. Whatever it is, it will be okay." You had me when I was a crying waitress and you should have known that, I should have told you that. But you didn't and I didn't.

THE ART TEACHER

In his book, *The Disappointment Artist*, Jonathan Lethem says that he learned to think by watching his father paint. When I read that sentence, my first thought was: I learned about love by listening to my mother sing along to "The Art Teacher" by Rufus Wainwright. My mother used to play it loudly at our little house in the woods and yell along to the lyric: *Never have I loved since then. Never have I loved ANY OTHER MAN!*

I liked the passion that my mother yelled with. I think it was then that the idea got into my head that I wanted a lover to shake me up so much that I could never love any other man. I don't think my mom was actually singing about any particular man. In my mind as a kid though, she was.

In 1973 my mom saw Rufus's mother, Kate McGarrigle, at the Buffalo Folk fest pregnant with Rufus in her stomach. She was wearing overalls that covered her belly bump. My mom says that's when her infatuation began. "She was so adorable," my mom told me.

I remember singing along with her to "The Art Teacher" while she did dishes at the kitchen sink, while she shifted gears with me in the passenger seat of our hatchback, while we ate Popsicles on the couch, and while she put make-up on (my dad called it "putting her face on") in the bathroom.

I remember when my mother actually was in love with her art teacher. It was summer and I was fourteen. No, I'm exaggerating. She couldn't have been in love, no way, just attracted to him. I don't know, I'll ask her.

But one afternoon, before she was off to her pastel class, I walked into the bathroom and my mom was pulling her hair back. She looked in the mirror and put one hand up flat, pretending it was paper and used her right hand to pretend to sketch. Her eyes glanced down and then back up to the mirror a few times. "What are you doing?" I asked. "I want to see what I look like from my teacher's perspective when I draw," she said to my friend and me. We promptly burst out laughing.

Another time, when I was snooping around her email, I read some emails that seemed quite risqué but they weren't from her art teacher. They were from her yoga teacher. I can't make this stuff up.

"The Art Teacher," in my opinion, is one of the greatest, yet eeriest, love songs. I've played it for a few other people and they weren't nearly as impressed as me. Maybe it's too feminine, too cerebral. It really does it for me. Partly, because it reminds me of my mother. Partly because I love Rufus's voice and his piano playing. And then there are the words.

There I was in uniform
Looking at the art teacher
I was just a girl then
Never have I loved since then

Okay so, imagine Rufus as a young lad, in his school uniform, ogling his sexy art teacher. If that's not enough to get your blood pumping, I don't know what is.

I was just a girl then. It's gorgeous. A grown man calling himself a girl, then. Between his sentences, Rufus sucks in these deep and desperate breaths through his teeth. It really adds to the intensity.

A few years ago, I was sitting with a man I loved in my mother's living room. It was the first time he came to my childhood home. We made coffee in a little pot though it was almost evening. It was fall. We were alone. My mother has a good music collection and we decided to each choose a song to play for one another. He chose "Man in the Shed" by Nick Drake.

But the man is me, yes and the girl is you
So leave your house come into my shed
Please stop my world from raining through my head

You know what I choose. He was quiet while listening to it, sipping his coffee.

"Do you get it?" I pressed. "Are you listening?"

"Yeah," he said slowly, thinking. "Pant-suit sorta thing... never loved any other man...Jesus. Wow." I knew he would sense the power of the song just as I could. We argued about lots of things, but music wasn't one of them. With music we rarely went wrong.

After doing some research, it turns out that I've been taking the song too literally. According to most people, Rufus thought it would be fun to write a song from the perspective of a schoolgirl. I still like to think he is talking about himself. That's the beauty of songs, though, the beauty of books, the beauty of interpretation. We can listen to things and choose to interpret them in the way that make us feel the least alone, or the way that entertains us most. I like songs like "The Art Teacher" which, in four minutes, I feel like I've read a story. I've been sucked into this child's life—this child that turns into an adult with a broken heart. I feel like I've listened to a well-written essay wherein I was given the creative freedom to fill in my own gaps.

But mostly I related because I know that I would have bought a painting I didn't love, if someone I was in love with loved it.

HUNGER

I had this boyfriend once who cooked for a living and he swore by putting blue cheese on hamburgers. I consider it when I go to order a burger but then I feel like—no, no—that's what a fat ass would do, and I hold off. It's too decadent of a thing. I know those blue cheese calories aren't going to put me over the edge, but still.

Lauren—my best friend—and I, we went to an orgy together last fall. At the time I was in a non-conventional and highly sexual relationship with an older man. I'd recently read a memoir about a woman's sexual experiences as a teenager in Italy. My lover knew I was obsessed with one scene in which the protagonist is blindfolded and then surrounded by four men who take turns tapping her on the head and then putting their cock in her mouth. She never sees the men. It was within that context which I received a text message from him reading: "Come suck our dicks in the dark." I was turned on and excited but was at a party playing beer pong with Lauren, so I told him I could go the next night—but only so long as Lauren could come.

Initially, Lauren felt apprehensive about participating in the orgy but she is also the friend that will do anything for me because we are a little bit in love with one another. Later,

I would feel bad about dragging her to the orgy, and I would remember the morning of the motel, when I saw her with her arms crossed in her new fuchsia silk robe staring out the window with a blank look into the late October sky and saying she was going to go take a long shower. She said she felt dirty.

I didn't feel dirty. I felt horny.

Lauren and I got ready for the orgy in my bathroom together in the way that girl best friends get ready together. She straightened the parts of my hair for me that I could not reach and she did my eye makeup because (even though she says she is not)—she is better at doing eye make-up than I am. Our outfits mimicked each other with variations of black fishnet tights, form fitting black dresses and combat boots. We looked like perfect sluts. Like pre-teens allowed to go to the movies alone for the first time and discovering their sexuality. On our way out the door, we had to walk by my dad, sitting at the table paying his bills. He asked us where we were going. "A Halloween party," I said. I did not feel my age. I felt ten.

We took Lauren's minivan to the motel in White Plains. She drove and I sat shotgun. It was the time of the year when it was starting to get dark early and it makes your serotonin low. We stopped at a gas station for a bag of pretzel rods and cigarettes even though neither of us smokes. We were listening to Damien Marley. I was edgy and she was edgy and we barely spoke. Nerves. I kept thinking I lost the directions but I'd be sitting on them or they'd be in my other hand. The van was packed with handcuffs, blood paint, her guitar, my keyboard, glitter, and a piñata in the shape of a black cat filled with condoms and candy.

It was a two-hour ride and about halfway through we stopped at McDonald's to get Coca-Colas. Our plan was to drink the Cokes halfway down and then fill the rest of the cup with the scotch I'd brought along. After some sips of our beverages we relaxed a bit. But then the rain started in, the sun was completely down and again I lost the directions. I turned the music down.

"Sorry, dude, that Damien Marley is really stressing me out right now."

"You don't think I'm stressed out dude? It's raining, we're lost, I'm drunk and I'm driving you to a goddamn orgy that I'm still on the fence about."

Terrified she was going to turn the car around, I shut up and tried to radiate good energy. Eventually we made it, parked, and busted into the motel.

We brought various outfits to wear in case we felt inspired to do some role-play throughout the night. We'd gone to Wal-Mart and bought athletic shorts, wife beaters on which we'd painted big ORGY '09s, and soccer socks. Oh, and footie pajamas. Yes. Lauren's were green with dinosaurs and mine (borrowed from her) were purple with pink owls.

The best part of an orgy is sitting on your knees wearing owl-print footie pajamas next to your best friend wearing green dinosaur print footie pajamas, alternating cocks to suck.

That sounds weird but if you were there, it was actually a really gentle and tender thing. I sound sarcastic. I can assure you I am not. We brought a laptop to the orgy. We went to YouTube. Lauren had the idea to listen to "Judy Blue Eyes" by Crosby, Stills, Nash and Young. When the "do do do do doot do do do do do do" part came, we all stopped.

Danced. Snapped. Sang. Clapped. Smiled. Switched cocks. Sucked. Came. Breathed. Laughed. Lauren and I kissed a little. Beautiful. It was possibly one of the best eight minutes and forty-one seconds of my life. The closest I have ever felt to living during the sixties.

I've always liked sucking cock. It's a safe place. I close my mind and open my mouth. There is no external monologue dribbling out. It shuts me up. Except, I will admit, I am a girl who talks and laughs through sex and blowjobs. I'll stop to change the music. I'll have to show you this part of a book. I'll have to take my gum out and put it on a book. I'll have to turn the music up. Then down. Then up. I'll take my mouth off of your cock to say, "That was so funny ten minutes ago when my roommate was like blah blah blah and you were like blah blah." I am waiting to meet a guy who tells me to shut up. But it seems I only sleep with nice guys.

The other great thing about having an orgy is the guilt-free blue cheese burger you can eat afterward, because you feel thin. I mean, like, an enormous juicy bacon cheeseburger cooked medium well to well with the blue cheese dressing slavered over it. Onions and lettuce and tomatoes. Fries—you can have the fries—don't substitute the fries for a side salad they will charge you an extra three dollars for even though it is primarily made up of iceberg lettuce. You should put the fries *on* your burger. Maybe swig a malted milkshake. I mean—I usually feel sort of thin after just *sex*. So you can imagine how skinny I feel after an orgy.

If I'm totally honest: my favorite part of the orgy was the part where one guy was fucking me from behind and the other guy's cock was deep in my mouth.

Lauren says that if she is totally honest, her favorite part of the orgy was when our plastic sword with fake blood in it exploded from stabbing the piñata and the fake blood got all over the motel rug.

And Lauren says the best thing to eat after an orgy is a tuna melt with cheddar cheese on rye. Lauren is a semi-vegetarian. She was a full vegetarian for quite a few years, until I dared her to eat some bacon with me at a diner once and she did it. I don't know what the fuck you would eat after an orgy if you were a full vegetarian. Garden burger I guess. Stir-fry doesn't have the same ring to it.

I am not a big eater. I like to eat, but I am a lazy eater. I am not skinny. I am average—one-hundred and thirty-seven pounds or something, not that I'm counting. I am lying. In the house where I work there is a digital scale. I weigh myself every day but mainly for amusement. But I am talking about the *feeling* of post-sex slenderness.

There are times I overexert myself sexually just so I can overeat the next day. I remember there were a few times in New York when I had so little money, and I would be having sex with my lover through the night—all the while looking forward to the morning because I was planning on getting stoned and treating myself to some incredible egg and cheese and bacon sandwich and orange juice and coffee. Then I remember thinking it was really pathetic that I was thinking that during sex and how I must be really hungry.

Right now, for example, I am shoving food in my mouth— a bean and cheese frozen burrito and an Apricot Ale. It tastes good, I guess, but I don't deserve the calories. I didn't have an orgy tonight, today, or yesterday or last month. My life is progressing and not progressing. I'm not sore. I don't have any bruises. It doesn't hurt when I pee. No scratches. Lauren and I agree on this. Once we were getting back to the van after a four hours steep hike and she said, "I'm into deserving calories."

Another fun part during an orgy is hearing one guy say:

"Watch her tits, watch them bounce. Those are youuuuuunnnng tits."

Then the other guy echoes: "Youuuuuunnnng tits"

They were fondling them and even thinking about it right now makes me want to masturbate.

I know a lot of the sentences verbatim from the orgy because I have it on tape. I tape-recorded the entire orgy. I honestly think it is my greatest work of art. When I took the airplane out here to the west coast the day after the orgy, I listened to the tape with headphones and made myself come almost instantly under those navy blue blankets they give you on airplanes. The man next to me was snoring.

When Lauren and I left the love fest in the morning we drove to a diner she knew off the Thruway. We had the orgy burger and the orgy tuna melt. I tried to talk Lauren into getting blue cheese on her tuna melt but she said that would be gross. We didn't talk much—mostly looked out the window at the old men and their motorcycles. After our plates were cleared, Lauren looked at me and said she would "probably never do anything like this again."

We left the diner and drove back to our neck of the woods. Not wanting to go home quite yet, Lauren drove us down to the railroad tracks on the Hudson River. Lauren keeps a futon mattress in the back of her minivan and so we slept in the sun side by side for a few hours. Our arms were touching. I woke up drenched in sweat and miserable. The minivan was moving.

Lauren wasn't next to me anymore. She was driving. She saw I was awake and because she is my best friend she immediately saw I was depressed and she told me not to get up, she told me to lie back down, and she said, "Just pretend you're on a magic carpet."

I pretended I was on a magic carpet. And for a moment, everything felt better.

BERLIN: STRANGE LIKE THE MUSIC OF THE DOORS

Everyday in Berlin is Saturday, the melting pot of people at the park tell me. *No, everyday in Berlin is an existential crisis,* I would like to correct them. I smile and nod. I take a sip of my 65-cent Sternburg beer and I pretend to love Berlin like everyone else.

They tell me this to comfort me. But I see it as a warning and I begin to dread Saturdays.

"Have fun in Berlin!" the two girls I met at the bar yell to me as they leave. *No!* I want to yell back. The girls are so friendly. They remind me of my old self. I would be friends with them if I were in New York. They write their email addresses down in my journal and add: *email me for fun in Berlin!* Uh-huh.

CHRISTIAN ON THE SECOND FLOOR

My friend Lisa and I sublet a room at 30 Boxhagner Strasse. While buying beer across the street at the Kiosk one night we meet the guy that lives the floor below us. We sing Suzanne Vega to him: "My name is Christian. I live on the second floor. I live upstairs from you. Yes I think you've seen me before."

The three of us become inseparable because the three of us are inconsolably depressed. The week before Christian met us, his girlfriend left him and he tried to kill him self and woke up in a hospital. Even though it's summer, we stay inside most days and pass joints back and forth. Sometimes we watch three movies a day. Movies like: *Sid and Nancy*, *Wristcutters: A Love Story*, and *Suburbia*. Christian feeds us Kinder chocolate bars and gummy candy called Happy Cola. He says he can't be bothered to cook anymore. I feel fat. We eat fruit salad every day, sometimes twice. When three miserable people make fruit salad it consists of one apple and one banana. Once we ate it with a grapefruit. Once.

THE KIOSK

I stare out the window in Christian's apartment like if I do it long enough I will forget or remember things. In the corner of his bedroom, you can take a step up to an alcove with windows for walls and can see three different street corners. There I stare, stoned, at dogs off of leashes, purple dreadlocks, pink and blue sky, electric blue rat-tails, red mohawks, and camouflage shorts. I stare at people holding beers in one hand and babies in the other. Mostly I study the people at the kiosk across the street. There are three guys who have grown up in Berlin, that stand there all day. I like to imagine what they talk about. They stand there nursing beers from the afternoon until dawn. I never see them arrive and I never see them leave. I talk in my head to New York. New York, I am hoping for an experience that pre-dates you—that cancels you out. I know I won't have this experience if I keep staring out the window growing a beer gut, but I have no reason to stop. I stare out the window and think about how

I am starting to gain weight from doing nothing but staring out the window. In the kitchen, I can hear a German man making pasta. I remember feeling like I'd attempted suicide and failed. Like I'd thrown my life off of a bridge to drown it but it fucking floated. In the background, Christian listens to a song on repeat that goes:

I wanna do crack cause you're never coming back, I wanna shoot speedballs, bang my head against the wall, I wanna sniff glue cause I can't get over you, am I gonna sort it out?

BOXHAGENER PLATZ-PARK

Say the name of a drug you want in Berlin and it will be in your hand the same day. The park is full of strange men and women. We give them all nicknames: *Is that the Tunisian PCP guy? Is that the demon Nazi guy? Hey, there's white shirt dance man. Is that the punk?* We don't know their names and they don't know ours. But until the pre-dawn we all sit together in a circle, lit with tea lights and dogs and hash and guitars and bottles.

Lisa and I are sitting on the swings at night when a girl with long brown hair, about thirty years old, comes up to us.

"Would you like to share my speed with me?"

"Sure..."

We blow speed off of the History book that she uses in her classroom. "I'm a *teacher* now, you know?" she kept saying. "So don't tell anyone I do speed."

We talked about communism and the upcoming German elections. She mostly preached. She was disturbed we didn't speak much German.

"But you know that *we* can speak English right?" she asked.

"I'm aware of that."

"I'm doing speed now because my mom died," she said.

Pain feels the same in every country.

NEW YORK

It's five in the evening and Lisa and I have just woken up even though we went to bed at midnight. Seventeen hours. Getting up to do nothing is hard. The sun is gentle and we are in the kitchen. I am staring out the window at The Kiosk. Lisa is sitting on the windowsill smoking a cigarette. Berlin is compressed of all the days off that we wished for in New York. They make me want to die.

"I'm thinking about making tea," I say to Lisa.

"I'm thinking about going back to New York," she says.

"I'm thinking about that too," I respond.

"I think I might have pissed the bed last night," she says.

STEPHANIE FRASKEN

A woman named Stephanie Frasken hires me to clean her flat once a week. I spend the money I earn on beer and speed. I like Stephanie more than anyone else I have met in Germany because I can scrub her toilet and she generously pays me in euros. She is from Los Angeles and smokes Marlboro lights and simultaneously does yoga and talks on her headset. She has a Buddha statue from Target. She can't clean her own toilet. Her life seems sad to me. One morning while I am still on acid, I go to the computer to email her that I won't be able to make it. She'd sent me an email that she loved my eager and earnest attitude and could I start coming three days a week? I couldn't even write back because I couldn't figure out how to use a keyboard and Christian had turned into an evil white bunny rabbit that I thought was conspiring against me.

THE GIRL FROM BARCELONA WHO SPEAKS CHINESE

I have fallen in love with a girl named Tau, rhyming with cow. Tau would consider herself a freegan if she considered herself anything but she doesn't believe in considering. Tau has dark eyelashes and olive skin. Small boned but not bony. She reminds me of a beautiful child. Tau lives in a place called The Caravan with fifteen other people. There is one bedroom with fifteen mattresses. The door of The Caravan is spray painted green and orange and reads: *WELCOME. WE DON'T KNOW WHAT IS GOOD FOR YOU.* The other side of the door says: *YOU ARE WELCOME EVERYDAY AND ON SATURDAY.* I am sometimes in love with my female friends but I never want to touch them the way I wanted to touch Tau. When I sat next to her one evening, our bare knees, shoulders and arms touching, I felt like a man: completely infatuated with her face and body.

Tau says shaving is shameful. She doesn't shave her armpits or legs. Tau says she hasn't watched a television in three years. Tau says she found photography at age thirteen and believed that it was all she needed. She says she thinks she conceives life differently from others and she wants to actually bring this difference to reality. Tau speaks Spanish, English, Chinese and German. I speak English.

I told Tau I don't believe in privacy anymore. She told me she wants to live in a glass house where people can watch her have sex, brush her teeth and eat breakfast. "Are we crazy and we don't know it?" She asked me, grinning.

MORBID

"Christian?" I ask. He is getting dressed for therapy. He is in a good mood because his therapist is really hot and "keen on chemicals and putting them together like Lego blocks," and he was going to get some "high-end Prozac type feel good shit."

"Yes?"

"If you were to kill yourself, how would you do it?"

"With a bang."

"With a gun?"

"Pistols are hard to get here in Germany and shit… but yeah."

*

My brother and I are laying across from each other on couches in West Berlin. I am looking at the clock that runs backwards and thinking about how that clock is like my life, regressing.

"Trev, when you die, where do you want your ashes scattered?"

"I don't know. I don't care. But wherever you do it, plant tomatoes. Then I could live inside tomatoes. That would be cool."

*

Lisa can't sleep and I hear her click her lighter and her Camel Light wafts in the hot air.

"Lisa-bird?"

"Chlo-bird?"

"If you were to die tomorrow, what would you want it to say on your gravestone?"

"I don't know. Maybe something like, 'I wasn't fucking stupid, dude. I was just curious.'"

GERMAN ACID

Was pretty much the same as American Acid except it lasted longer and felt stronger. My heels were black and I thought they could never be white again.

"Trips aren't supposed to last longer than twelve hours," Christian told me from the computer desk.

"How long has it been?" I asked.

"Eighteen hours. *Oh, don't DO THAT, MAN!*"

"What? WHAT?"

"I am talking to Backpack Man. He has these creepy fingers he is waving to me and shit?"

"I'm seeing flamingoes," I said.

Hours, (minutes?) later, Christian was on his side, his back to me. His shoulders were trembling.

Oh, fuck, I thought. I am tripping with a crying German man. But I didn't ask him if he was crying because I didn't know what to do if he was crying.

Hours, (minutes?) passed and I became curious.

"Hey, were you crying before?"

"No. I was laughing at this pear."

I cannot describe the profound relief I felt that I wasn't hallucinating the pear. I didn't even ask where or how he was seeing it. I didn't open my eyes. I didn't want to see it. I had seen enough. But then ten minutes later I got curious again.

"This pear?"

"What?"

"You said were laughing at this pear? Where?"

"This *pear.*"

"Yeah, I know. Where are you seeing it?

"Seeing what?"

"This pear. What pear?"

"Are you fucking with me? This *pear.* I don't know how to pronounce it in English."

"…Liz Phair?"

"No, man, you know when you are scared and shit? *Dis*pear"

"Despair! Oh my god. I thought you were laughing at this pear."

"I was laughing in despair."

As we came down, we watched *The Simpson's* in German and I couldn't stop laughing. We lit tea lights. Then I took the best shower of my life while Christian went to the Kiosk to get frozen pizzas with shrimp on them. We smoked joints and ate it in bed. I counted on my fingers. I was leaving Berlin in two days.

EXPIRED

I kept my MetroCard in the right pocket of my black leather jacket the four months that I lived in Berlin. I rubbed it like a worry stone. I obsessively checked for it. I just wanted to get back to MetroCard land. The night before I left Berlin, Lisa told me to take her Metro card. Then I had two.

The morning I left, my brother told me to take his Metro card. I had three. When I got to Penn Station, they all had insufficient funds. When I got to Penn station, it was after midnight and I missed my train to go upstate and the next train didn't run until six in the morning. When I got to Penn Station, I realized I had nowhere to go in New York City and no cell phone. When I got to Penn Station, I had to spend the night there, which was worse than any bad acid trip.

UNDERGROUND

On the G train we fall asleep touching, my head on your shoulder, and you slur and say, "At least we have each other," and I say, "What?" and you say, "At least we have each other," and I say, "I was just going to say that."

On the G train in the mornings there is a woman crack-head who flicks her lighter at me and mutters about murdering me while I sit, trying to look composed and unphased and unafraid, wearing black and white, writing in my journal on my way to waitress the brunch shift.

On the G train I take candy from a stranger. I can smell marijuana on him, and I know I should say no, but he has these sesame peanut butter things that look too good to pass up, and he offers them to me with such integrity that I take one. I take three of them. When I get home to Bushwick, I don't regret this and I eat the candies in my bedroom.

On the G train I am on Adderall writing in my journal and I remember that somewhere I read that writing in public makes people uncomfortable and I get sort of paranoid that I am making people uncomfortable because this is New York City and you don't want to mess around.

On the G train I tell you I have to get off because I am going to throw up. We get off a few stops before our own. I walk to the wall on the platform and slide down and put my head in my knees. You buy me a plain bagel and those mints I like from the bodega.

On the L train we meet a girl who is sick and mumbling to herself and tiny and we walk her to her apartment in Bushwick and later we tell people that we met a heroin angel.

On the L train you eat grapefruit and yogurt which are the opposite of train foods and it's really gross and people stare. You pose with your spoon in your hand and talk and talk, completely unaware.

On the L train I reach into my bag and find a piece of bread wrapped in aluminum foil. I look up at you and tell you I have bread in my bag and you shrug and say, "This is New York, who doesn't have bread in their bag?"

On the L train I often end up in the same car as the saxophone alien. He says, "Greetings Earthlings," in a mock robotic voice and then he announces that he will play his saxophone obnoxiously in our faces until we give him money to stop. It's brilliant. He even wears antennas. I pretend to be annoyed when I see him like everyone else but I secretly love it.

On the L train I discover that I left my purple wallet at the White Castle in Bushwick.

On the L train you say you are excited to see where I live. You say you like to be the first person to fuck me in all of my beds.

On the L train you teach me to play roulette. "As the subway slows, you look at the people waiting on the platform and make an educated guess of who you think will come into the car you're in. Or, another way to play is to choose which good looking guys you'd like to get on your car."

On the L train you ask me if we are under water now like in the Bright Eyes song "Train Under Water" and I say yes and you say that freaks you out. You say it makes you nauseous. We are standing and you moved to New York the day previous and you are on your way to your interview at the Strand.

On the L train we wear the straw hats we found on Avenue A.

On the L train you throw up in your hands from doing something we shouldn't have been doing.

On the J train we sit across from the cartoon drawing of a stick figure man littering with a line through it and you nudge me and say, "No throwing sugar cubes, dude."

On the A train I tell you to trade iPods with me because I want to see what you were listening to before you met up with me. "Safety Bricks" by Broken Social Scene.

On the A train it's the fourth of July and my roommate and I are wearing plastic ponchos and I tell my roommate that I'm terrified of lightning and my roommate tells me that smoking kills more people in a decade than lightning. She tells me that logic and anxiety rarely go together.

On the A train on the way to your apartment at two in the morning, I find the book *How To Further Your Intelligence*, and I can hardly believe my own luck. When I bring it into your apartment, you tell me I find things because I am looking for them.

On the A train I shave my legs somewhat dry because I saw another girl do it. On the A train we pound Jell-O shots that we took out of my refrigerator, left over from a Halloween party. It's Saturday and the train is going local. By the time we get to W. 4th, we are shitfaced.

On the A train I see a boy with Nike sneakers and backpack and I wish he would save me from myself.

On the A train there is a Mariachi band and they play "Here Comes the Sun." On the A train I read the back of a pregnancy test and eat Smart food popcorn.

On the A train your eyes look blood shot and happy and embarrassed when I slip you a hundred dollar bill out of the envelope my boss gave me with a cash bonus in it. You'd been complaining about how you couldn't afford a sweatshirt and you hadn't gone to a hair salon in a year. I shove it in your pocket when you got off on W. 4th Street. Later when I see you, you have a bright blue sweatshirt from American Apparel and short pink hair.

On the A train we sit side by side and you take out the Bible and I take out my journal. You laugh to yourself and say that you only took out the Bible to mess with me, but that's not true because even at home you've been reading the Bible. I take the top off of my marker and begin to write. "What's that smell?" you ask me.

On the 1 train we are going downtown and sharing headphones listening to "Fistful Of Love" by Antony And The Johnsons and you play the drums on the subway bars and my thighs and I feel overstimulated in this moment because that was always the song I said I wanted played at my future wedding.

On the 1 train you tell me that you like to look at different girls hands on the poles and imagine the pole as your cock.

On the R train we ride to the last stop in Brooklyn. Cheerleaders from the Midwest get on the train. One sits next to me and I talk to her. I ask her if she likes New York. When we walk up the stairs and to the street we stand on the pavement and you light a cigarette. I am a few feet across from you. You nod toward the pavement square I am standing on. "That's where my dad died," you say.

On all of the trains I wave enthusiastically to any babies that I see. I stick my tongue out and make faces and smile at them. I try to connect with them. "I always do this," I tell you.

On the L train I stand alone. On the G train I eat grapefruit. On the A train I try not to fall asleep but I learn to rest my eyes the way the rest of the adults do and I clutch my purse tightly while I do it. On the 1 train I look at different girls' hands and think of your hands.

THE SHIT YOU SAY

You say you're washing dishes and serving drinks at a bar in the Southernmost part of Australia. You say you're living in a camping trailer out back of the bar through a yard filled with dog shit and bones. You say it's white trash off an island of Tasmania. You sound angry. You say you are like a small retarded child crossing a busy highway and that I must hold your hand. You say, Jesus. You say, Jesus, you really had me going for the past few years. You say I am not who I say I am. Once you said you loved me "so much" but you never say that anymore. That was a one-time occasion that I remember with pathetic detail. You say you feel like you're the tortoise and I'm the hare. You say: Be careful with your drugs. You say: You can't write when you're dead. You say if I ever have the inclination, I should print out all of our emails. You say when you read our old Gchats it makes you want to kiss Google. You say if I ever have the inclination, I should watch the movie *Bob Le Flambeur*. I promised myself I would stop talking to you but I say why. You say the lead girl reminds you of me. I say why. Irreverent, you say. You look like her, you say. (You've always called me irreverent. You've branded me irreverent. In my mind you invented irreverent.) You say if I ever have the inclination, I should listen to the song, *Mountain Bed* by Wilco. You say you love it. You say it's beautiful. You say it's heartbreaking and I listen to it and agree.

You say you used to feel like you were with a wizened spiritual monk. You say you have now returned to that monk's hut, only to find the monk sitting in his underwear, smoking cigarettes and laughing his ass off while watching *Frasier*. You say the monk is me. I tell you I've never been a monk and that I have no idea what you're talking about.

You say you can't figure out why you're so gullible when it comes to me. You say it is very difficult not to respond to me. You say it's nearly impossible. You say I quickly become hurtful and mean. You say my feelings always change. They always do, you say. Re-send that email when you're not so manic, you say. Re-send that email when your feelings have changed. You say I dramatize people. You say I afford them qualities that they may or may not possess. You say I need to decide if I want you in my life or not. You need to decide! you yell, addressing me with my first name. You say that you don't know if it is a generational thing or what but that you are NOT ALWAYS PAYING ATTENTION TO YOUR FUCKING PHONE. You say yes, you are coming back to New York. You say maybe you will start sending me 6,000 emails a day the way I do to you. You say I've had a million phones since you've met me. You say that you can't help but feel that muses are real and that I am yours. You say you don't want to be left behind. You say that most people in the world are sheep but you don't think I am. You say you feel lost and lazy and self-absorbed and groping. You say you would never live with me because you would go crazy. You say you know what it's like to have leftover love. You say you hope that I don't give up on you completely. You say we've got something special between us and that we both know it. You say you think we will have joyous times again. You say you truly think so. You say I don't have to show my mom every single thing I write. You say I am going to become paralyzed from the way I crack my back. You say if we shared a desk we'd alternate fucking and arguing across it. You say you have highs and lows. You say you're sorry that you're so up and down. You say it seems like I am plugged into everything I am around. You say it's like we absorb one another. Then you say you don't know what you mean by that. You say will you shut up for one second. You say you don't remember what you were saying. You say you can't even hear your own brain. You say my eyes are blue even though I tell you they're green. You say you will put your dick in my armpit next time we have sex. I say what would be the point of that and you laugh and say, because it would be weird.

You said once, that a woman's body changes three times in her lifetime. My body was changing. My breasts were fluctuating. Months later, I bring that up to you and ask you to elaborate. You exhale your weed, giggle, and say, "What? I said that?" You shake your head and you say, "Maaaaaaaaaaaaaan. Jesus Christ. The shit I say."

LONG MAY YOU RUN

If you were born in May, I will probably rip pages of poetry out of books for you and put them in my pocket to give to you when I see you. I will steal books from the Strand bookstore and from the library for you. I will make you things, like journals and collages and animals out of Sculpey clay and I will clean my room when you come over. You will be the only reason I will ever clean my room. I will do drugs with you. I will give you a typewriter. I will not be able to keep my hands off of you. I will pick flowers and bring them to your windowsill. I will want to borrow your things. I will talk a lot around you because that is what I do around people I like. I will like you and I will maybe even love you. I will snoop through your shit and read your journals because I will think you are amazing and creative and communicative. I will pick fights with you out of insecurity and neuroses. I will want to break glass and crush flowers and kill you. I will move across the country to make sure I can live without you. I will move across the country to find you. I know it is rude to call people by numbers. But that is how I am doing this.

Number Five of May. I loved him because he was my older brother's friend. Because I met him a few hours after I moved to New York City and my life felt different. Because he had glasses. Because he made me an origami box to keep my jewelry in. Because he brought atlases to bars. Because he had an encyclopedia for a brain and a slim body. Because he only sat on floors and he only used pencils, never pens. Because he told me that if you live in New York, you live in dog years. Because he was right. Because he liked to play "follow the leader" and because he gave me a journal. Before Number Five moved back to the Midwest from New York City, I put my typewriter that he loved in the language section of the Strand bookstore where he worked with a typed note telling him I'd miss him. I spied on him, when he found it and he had a smile bigger than his face.

The Sixth of May was from San Diego. He was my room-mate in Washington Heights. It was New York hot. We had no air conditioner. We watched Sandy Kane on cable TV and took cold showers together late at night. We drank St. Ides forties and shared a mutual love for Elliott Smith. He made me laugh because he carried his stuff around in a plastic bag. Number six was sharp, sharp, sharp and sarcastic. He reminded me of Will from Will and Grace. He read a lot of Salinger and he ate a lot of Chinese food. He walked around in his underwear often and had a lithe body. He'd go get us bagels and Plan B in the mornings. During sex, Number Six asked me if he could slap me and I said no. Then I changed my mind and said yes.

Number Eight is hard to talk about and not just because he is dead because even when he was alive, he was hard to talk about. He was a boy with a ponytail and a Tom Waits T-shirt. We ate each other alive for a while. We scarfed Wonder Bread and snorted heroin for a while. He wrote a song for me and recorded it onto a cassette tape with a handmade cover. He let me keep his copy of *Junky*. Number Eight had the perfect penis. Slightly curved. Number Eight said he had a monkey on his back. That he felt like Einstein selling hot dogs. That he was the only asshole in New York with any umbrella etiquette. That I should respect myself more. Number Eight died on the eighth. I don't know if I ever loved him. I just know that I wanted to be him. I just know that some days I want to drink a bottle of liquor and roll around on his grave. The last time I saw The Legendary (as he called himself) Number Eight, we made a painting together. We sat on our knees in the dim kitchen with full glasses of red wine and small bottles of paint. I followed his lead. I spilled my wine on the canvas. He said who cares. There was music on and he leaned forward and kissed my forehead. The night Number Eight died, I brought the painting outside and left it on the street corner.

I sleep and wake up well next to Number Nine. Number Nine and I try to align our breathing. Number Nine is new and current in my life, so it is hard to know what to say about him yet. Number Nine is nice and gives hand massages. Number Nine tells me I am very beautiful. Number Nine likes to drink pitchers of beer while making many ambitious to-do lists and goal lists. We get on because I like doing those things too. We spent one Saturday making lists and origami frogs and eating chicken wings. We woke up on Sunday and had sex to the Beatles radio show. Number Nine likes to dance and has great teeth. I feel like I am ruining things with number nine before they even begin because I have showed him I'm crazy too early. Number Nine has glasses and sort of looks like Number Five, and on the first day we met, I told him that.

Ever since I got back from my visit to New York, Number Thirteen has been very affectionate. He takes my hand now when I see him like he is scared I am going to go away again. He never used to hold my hand. When he met me at the airport, he asked, "Were you sad?" I asked him why I would be sad and he said, "Because you didn't get to see me for a while." He holds my hand now even while we are just having milkshakes and french fries side by side at Scooter's Burgers looking out the window to Market Street. That's

what we were doing yesterday when "Time Of The Season"
by the Zombies came on and I remembered that that was
one of number eight's favorite songs. I felt pre-menstrual
and had watery eyes and Number Thirteen kept holding my
hand and asked me why I was sad and told me that he loved
me. Number Thirteen doesn't care what anyone thinks. He
wears a Spiderman costume—mask included—and carries a
sword around with him most days of the week. He says he
will protect me from the bad guys. He likes me to pretend
I am Cinderella for him. Over the milkshakes, Number
Thirteen told me he thinks vaginas are weird because they
look like small butts but triangular, and he is very happy
to have a penis instead. He asked me if I was sad to have a
vagina. I said yes, that sometimes it sucks. He asked me if I
hate it. I told him he shouldn't use the word hate. He told
me I shouldn't use the word sucks. Number Thirteen recently
turned four.

Number Sixteen is a chewing gum enthusiast, a pyroma-
niac, a photographer and a pothead. He sends me the up
and coming kinds of gum—like the one that changes from
fruity to minty—in Ziploc bags. I like to think that Number
Sixteen and I have a bond that runs deep even though we
only see each other once a year now, if we are lucky. The last
time I saw Sixteen we walked barefoot around Boston smoking bowls in a rainstorm.

Nineteen was my first May love. His name was Cameron but
he changed it to Kamaran. We met at guitar camp. We were
fifteen. I thought he was cool because he was getting eman-
cipated from his parents. He truly believed that he was John
Lennon reincarnated. We bought Coricidin Cough & Cold
and popped eight of them each and that was the first time
I tripped. There was something about his eyes—something
that was so important to me and now I don't remember.
Maybe one eye was lazy. Color blind? Two different colors?
Not sure. But I was completely in love with Kamaran. The
camp lasted two weeks. My dad picked me up and I sobbed

through the two-hour drive home. I was on that Coricidin kick and got a few of my friends to do it with me. They hated me for it. Four years later Number Nineteen contacted me when I lived in the city. His email address was lennon1969. He asked me to meet him at Grand Central Station. I spotted him from a distance. He was with his Mom.

Twenty-two is my bravest number. Twenty-two is brave because he handles me and I am learning that I am hard to handle. He hasn't walked away and maybe he should have. Actually, once he did start walking away, on my birthday, when I picked a fight, but then he remembered my phone was charging at his apartment and he claims that is the only reason he came back. Another time he drove away angry on his motorcycle, so I flew away to Berlin for a few months. But we always come back. We just keep ramming together, he says. I could swallow number Twenty-two in one gulp. Number Twenty-two and I met at a Monday night memoir writing class during the winter. I loved his writing. I asked him how he could write like that. I wanted to write like that. A special thing happened that winter. Things aligned. We listened to "Jigsaw Falling Into Place" by Radiohead a lot. The special thing kept happening through the spring, summer, fall and following winter. We listened to "Waterloo Sunset" by the Kinks a lot. Everything was eerily romantic. I am always writing with number twenty-two in mind. My number twenty-two is my best friend. He calls me his sex fantasy robot. His muse. We have an intensity you can hold in your hand, that you can pick up and put down. Sometimes Twenty-two's love is the only love that matters to me.

Number Twenty-three was my bartender. Number Twenty-three is Irish and likes the Pogues. Number Twenty-three dresses very odd. He wears pins on his T-shirts. He wears Pogues T-shirts. Number Twenty-three turned me on to a beer that he described as tasting like bananas and cloves. I became heavily addicted to the beer. Franziskaner. Number Twenty-three refilled my beer free of charge every time it was a quarter of the way down. I lived at that bar. Number Twenty-three told me I gave him indecent thoughts. I think Number Twenty-three reminded me of Number Twenty-two. And I am always looking for another twenty-two. I moved to a different neighborhood so number Twenty-three is not my bartender anymore.

Number Twenty-eight is the only person that ever came on my face. This makes him important, in a way, because it makes me remember him yet nothing else about him is worth remembering. Number Twenty-eight and I got into an embarrassing public spat at a bar, (the bar that Number Twenty-three is a bartender at) about Twitter. I was against it. He was for it and had good reasons to back it up. He said he couldn't believe how passionate I was about detesting Twitter. We didn't talk for a long time after that. Now we talk again and to my chagrin I am passionately pro Twitter.

CALL ME SOMETIME

My lover called today from a sunny field in Tennessee where he was smoking a cigar and drinking a bottle of absinthe, his typewriter and bicycle in tow.

My lover called today and we repeated a conversation about teeth and dental insurance and getting older and then we repeated a conversation about how we repeat stuff.

My lover called today and we interrupted each other a lot and talked in circles and went off on tangents.

My lover called today and I knew it was going to be him because my phone sounded abnormally eager when it rang.

My lover called from the S   outh today and I was sitting at an outdoor café on Bedford Avenue drinking mimosas in October and I didn't let him get a word in edgewise because I was drunk on love and life and I had just bought a brass necklace that said *Brooklyn*.

My lover called from New York today and I was outside my condominium in Seattle in the alley and it was pouring and I cried to him that I missed him and did not know what to do with my life and a few days later I got an email with some ideas of what to do with my life.

My lover called today and I hit ignore, so he called again and I hit ignore and one more time and I hit ignore because I was scared of him and didn't want to hear him yell at me.

My lover called today and said, "Waking up in the rain and drinking beer and playing drums makes me miss you. Now I'm going to eat my peanut butter and jelly sandwich on English muffin bread with a banana and kiwi and watch this British mini series called *Red Riding Trilogy* about murders and rain."

My lover called tonight and left me a voicemail telling me that I fucked it up. That we had our great times but that I fucked it up. That I was looking for the prize that didn't exist. I listened to the voicemail on speakerphone with my friends in a taxi on the way home and sobbed and held their hands.

My lover called today while I was driving a car through Hudson, New York, and I told him I was scared of being alone and he asked, "But when have you been?"

My lover called tonight and read to me from a Herman Hesse book.

My lover called tonight and read to me from *Whom The Bell Tolls.*

My lover called from upstate tonight and read to me from his journal with a sentence about me that read, "I love every-thing about you."

My lover called this morning to tell me he is back in therapy.

My lover called me this evening when I got home from work and told me he went to bed thinking of me.

My lover called today while I was getting low-lights in my hair at a place called Vain.

My lover called from his East Village stairs this morning ignoring the three-hour time difference and when I answered with a raspy hello he yelled "Gooooood morning!" in my ear and it was a happy way for me to wake up.

My lover called today and for the first time he said, "I love you so much," instead of "I love you."

My lover called this morning when I was in my Green-point apartment and told me he smashed into a taxi when he left my apartment the night before.

My lover called today when I was in Hudson working at my dad's store in the basement and my dad brought me the phone and I lay down on the cement and put my hand between my legs.

My lover called today when I was in his apartment and he was at a rest stop on his motorcycle and told me he couldn't take my ups and downs anymore.

My lover called tonight and left me a voicemail, yelling, "Fuck me? *Fuck you*!"

My lover called today and said he has a cold and is smoking the rest of his weed and watching Netflix.

My lover called today to tell me he is starting a story about his back hair but then he had to get off the phone because the cable guy got there.

My lover called today from a motel in Winchester, Virginia because his motorcycle that he calls "Night Wing" broke down on his way to Tennessee.

My lover called tonight, drunker than I had ever heard him, and said things to me that matter and meant so much that I promptly forgot them.

My lover called tonight from Youngsville, New York, while I was outside in Seattle sitting on a stoop that was not mine, near a box of free eggplant, and he invited me to his mom's house for Christmas.

My lover called from the East Village tonight and I was in bed with my computer. I read to him a love letter I'd been working on for him called *The Cat and the Stream.*

My lover called today after I told him I read all of his private journals and he told me that I should leave his apartment. "I think you should leave," he said.

My lover called from his stoop on East Ninth Street and told me about a threesome gone wrong that he had with his Haitian weed dealer and his Haitian weed dealer's girlfriend.

My lover called to tell me the book *The Ethical Slut* hit a nerve in him.

My lover called while I was locking up my bike and told me that I have no idea how good he can be to me.

My lover called and told me he will hunt me down wherever I am.

My lover called and asked me what he would do without me.

My lover called today from the grocery store where he was buying a twelve pack of Blue Moon.

My lover called today and I went into the concrete basement for some privacy and my lover said he was en route to Brooklyn and I said are you going to go see your other lover and he said yes and I hung up the phone.

My lover called today and I was so distraught to hear his voice that I immediately afterwards rolled TOP tobacco and made a pot of tea and stared out the window.

My lover called today and sounded like he was crying but really he had just taken a huge rip from his bong. He said he'd been in bed all morning smoking weed and drinking cans of Budweiser.

My lover called from a laundromat in Brooklyn today. He said we hadn't talked on the phone in a while. He said he'd been having dreams about me. He said, "Am I on speaker phone?" and I said, "Yes, I'm brushing my teeth," and he said he didn't feel comfortable on speaker phone. Before we hung up, he told me he was proud of me, and that he would buy my book, because his unemployment check came through.

I moved to Washington and he moved to Tennessee. I moved to Hudson and he moved to Australia. I went to Portland and he went to Brooklyn. Eventually I stopped counting the time difference on my fingers. Eventually I stopped expecting the phone to vibrate. I began leaving it on the desk instead of under my pillow when I went to sleep. I stopped remembering to pay my bill on time or charge my phone.

Eventually, he stopped calling.

LEGS

Yes. It was starting again, the blood humming. She let it carry her. What was that Oscar Wilde quote?—that the beauty of the emotions is that they lead us astray.
—Susan Minot

My mother used to grab and squeeze my thigh, calling it a chunk of cheese. I feel like she only stopped doing that recently. My mother has great legs, and even better calves. I mean, enviable calves. I think it's because when she lies in bed she flexes and points for like ten minutes each night and each morning. She has naturally soft legs, no varicose veins and nice knees. She's fifty-six and they're still the absolute best part of her body. When I was a kid, and my parents had other couples over for dinner, my mom would drink red wine and once it hit her system, she'd become very competitive, challenging people to leg wrestle with her on the rug.

I was, I am, more of an upper body person. I can make my stomach pretty flat in a couple days with a Pilates video and the right foods. Shoulders, arms, tits, stomach. I do not rule the legs. I always hated my legs. I thought they were fat. In middle school, when the weather became warm enough for shorts, I remember being really stressed out—I would shave my legs, lotion them, put fake tanning products on them. While doing this routine one night, I remember my mom saying from the couch, "Wow, you really take wearing shorts seriously."

Anytime I've asked a man what their favorite part of my body was, they said, "Your stomach area." They like the piercing. My mother took my best friend Mary and I to get out belly buttons pierced when we were around fifteen. I'm surprised yet not surprised she let us do that. I must have begged her. It was summer, and afterwards she took some artsy close-up photographs of our stomachs.

Back to my own legs. My legs were eager to go to pre-school. You had to be two years and nine months to go. On the actual day I turned two years and nine months my mother tells me I ran into the school, sat in the circle, sang along, and didn't look back.

In Middle School, I remember shaving my legs with my best friend Mary. We sat on her blue tile bathroom counter with razors and Skintimate shaving cream and shaved a little at the ankle. Then a little more and a little more until we'd almost done the whole calf. It was so exciting. We went to bed that night, wondering if our mothers were going to be mad at us. We didn't talk about it then, but there was an air of suspense, like this was a new era of our lives. In the morning I went home, locked myself in the bathroom and finished the job. My mom was away that weekend, and I remember when she came home I was sitting on the corner of the couch with my knees tucked under a large sweatshirt and said, "Mom, I have to tell you something."

I've never broken a bone in my body. It makes me feel kind of like a pussy. I don't even have any cool scars on my legs. Though I do have a perfect circular freckle on the back of my right thigh. I remember lying in my mom's bed with her as a girl and her touching the freckle and saying, "Some man is gonna love kissing that beauty mark someday!"

Later, my legs were eager to leave high school. My legs walked the track in gym class instead of playing. My legs skipped out of school early to hit the gas pedal too aggressively and listen to Kanye West on tape in my Oldsmobile and to get high and drink coffee and smoke Parliament Light cigarettes.

So after graduation I went to Europe, lugged a huge suitcase through Barcelona and Paris and Sicily but I took birth control there and my tits blew up and I became so depressed and I ran out of money. I wanted to come home and after three months—I did. I went to Brooklyn.

I moved to Brooklyn and it was the pre-school thing all over again. My mother drove away and I didn't turn around to wave goodbye or watch the car disappear. My legs climbed onto the fire escape each morning with a cup of coffee. My heel kept time to songs by The Decemberists and Lily Allen and Regina Spektor and Belle and Sebastian. It was 2006.

My legs waitressed all day at an Israeli Café on Grand Street. Always on my fifth day of the workweek, I woke up on my mattress on the floor aching from the hips down. I waitressed in shoes I had to throw out constantly. Shoes that tore and flattened. Teal wedges and black Chinatown slip-ons and brown heeled cowboy boots. Once I was at work and those Chinese slip-ons broke and I stapled them back together.

When my mom came to visit, she'd be upset at the shoes my brother and I wore. You could almost see the entire side of his foot through his Converse and he even wore them through the winter. One time after my mother left, my brother and I were standing on the subway and he said to me, "Mom is weird. She thinks certain shoes like, make you healthy or something."

When I bought my first pair of Merrell's years later, not in New York, I realized she was right.

My legs stood on the L train, G train, one train, F train, A train and the 2 and 3 trains. My legs wandered Williamsburg and my legs rode this crappy blue bike I bought for twenty bucks on Bedford Avenue. My legs were often exhausted but in New York you don't really notice how exhausted you are until you leave and see that life in other places isn't so difficult and intense. It's funny—when I first got to New York, I felt found. Ever feel like you're in the exact right place at the exact right time? Ever feel like you're "following your heart," your legs? I was meeting people, a bunch of weirdoes, that liked me immediately. People I didn't know I needed to know.

What I am trying to say is that I was blown away. Didion says, "Quite simply, I was in love with New York. I do not mean 'love' in any colloquial way, I mean that I was in love with the city, the way you love the first person who ever touches you and you never love anyone quite that way again."

So I walked and walked, eavesdropped and observed, and then I found myself in a writing class with a man who made my legs weak and between my legs wet and after class at WXOU Radio Bar on Hudson Street, he put his hand on my thigh. That guy opened my legs even though he had a girlfriend he loved. One night he came back to my apartment after class and we sat on some stairs of an abandoned building in Brooklyn, drinking forties of Olde English and he said, "Don't fall in love with, me; I'm moving to Portland."

That was years ago.

The thing between my legs craved him like nothing I'd known before. I was consumed. The most joyous times of my life thus far were laughing with him between my legs.

Once we were walking on an upper catwalk in a subway station in Washington Heights, holding hands and he said, "I feel like a character from a book when I'm with you."

Once we were standing on top of a hill in the country in October. He handed me a flower and I put it in my flannel jacket.

Once we were walking to get ice cream cones from the window on Avenue A and we were talking about New York. Why we liked it. At the same time—synchronized—we both said: "I just like walking around."

Once we were walking around Greenpoint in the morning and looking at Manhattan from this junkyard. It was there that we said we swore we would be friends, we would write letters, we would keep things good, no matter how messy they would get. We didn't know. Or maybe we did.

One of the many times my legs ran up the seven flights to his apartment and I read aloud Bukowski's foreword in John Fante's *Ask The Dust*. He stood up and paced around excitedly and said, "You're like a cat that finds something and thinks it's cool and you want to show it to me because you know I'll think it's cool too, and you come dropping it off at my doorstep. This is why I love you." Then he gave me a kiss and a pair of his flannel pajama pants with snowflakes on them and I slept, in complete love.

I told what he said one night—the *don't fall in love with me* spiel—to a woman writer I know and she said, yeah, guys always say that—it's like saying: "Fall in love with me, but I'll make your life a living hell and you can't blame me because I told you not to."

To my chagrin, I obviously fell in love with him. And his legs never did get on that airplane to Portland.

But my own legs had this idea that getting on airplanes—that walking down ramp ways with a suitcase on wheels, that running away in a sense, would help me find whatever it was that I was looking for because he made it clear he could not give it to me. My legs were steps ahead of me—they were thinking maybe someone I could love lived on the West Coast. What if I was in the wrong place? I had to check. My legs wanted to open widely for someone new and have that person take his place—cancel him out. I wanted to feel far away from him. I wanted to feel the space.

I left for Seattle at four in the morning on Halloween. I said goodbye to my father in the predawn. When I talked to my brother on the phone a few days later, I asked how my dad was. "He said the funniest thing about you, the morning after you left," my brother said. "He said, 'I don't understand her. She's so casual.'" My brother and I cracked up.

In Seattle, I tried to try guys on, but I couldn't love any of them. Not like him.

One of those guys, the one I really really tried with, had a birthday party for me at his apartment in Bothell. In the morning I was sad, I was missing the man I loved in a deep way, and I gave him a blowjob in the AT&T parking lot where he worked. I kept my head down there for a long time. I had tears in my eyes. I was getting his cock as close to my ribs as I could. I was choking. When I took my head up, he asked me why I was crying.

I couldn't tell him, so he took me out for pancakes and eggs at iHop and didn't mind that I rudely read *The Worst Case Scenario Handbook* while we waited for our food. He even made light of it, saying things like, "Yeah, you should really read this urgent information right now, in case a black bear or a mountain lion runs in."

"We're in Bothell," I said, "There are only llamas," and he laughed and asked me why I was being so serious.

So my legs walked the ramp again. I flew back to the person I loved and hated the most. I knew he wasn't even in New York City anymore. But I figured that if I couldn't be with him, then at least I could be in the place where he had loved me.

My legs found yoga and they were happy doing downward dog splits and half crescent moon and lizard pose. The flexibility in my legs improved tremendously. My legs walked quickly through the autumn of New York City, waiting for him to come to me.

And he came; he always comes. And we had sex doggie-style on the floor of his friend's apartment and he told me my legs looked muscular, he told me I reminded him of his tenth grade girlfriend who was captain of the soccer team. "Have you been working out?" he asked me. He wanted me to keep my knee-high socks on. He wanted me to keep my brown lace-up boots on.

And we fell apart, we always do, we drank too much, we yelled and were mean and I laid next to him that night wanting to walk into the night.

One of last times we spoke was on the phone and I was pacing and I know he was pacing too. He is rarely still.

"I don't know how you could be so angry at me!" he said. "You break my heart!" he said.

"*You* broke *my* heart!" I said, "You broke my heart a million times. It hurts," I said. I said it three times as if each new utterance signaled another crack in my heart: "It hurts, it hurts, it hurts."

Once he told me I was like a river. I was sitting with my legs Indian style in bed. It was morning and he was putting his T-shirt on and going to work. It was the day after I got my tattoo. He laughed a little, I asked what, and he said, "I don't know…I just got this vision, this image of you. It was like you were running water—no, you were a stream, a stream or a river—and you were running through one part of my life into the next."

Then we went to my kitchen that had this seventies psychedelic flowered wallpaper and he opened my legs on the table.

TRUE LOVE

I gently told my cousin Henri, that I would have to leave Seattle. That I would be going back to New York for a while. I told him that New York was where my family and friends were, and that I missed them. We were sharing strawberry gelato on the patio of an Italian place we both love. He was four now, and I was twenty-four. Besides, I told him, New York is where the Teenage Mutant Ninja Turtles and Spiderman live.

Silence.

Then: "Well, then, you know what?"

"What?"

"Every morning when I get out of bed, I will probably cry."

"No. No, you won't. You'll be okay. And if you feel like you're going to cry, you can call me."

Silence.

"Okay?"

More silence, then: "Remember last time we were sitting here we saw those two dead crows?"

"Yeah. I remember that. And we named them Spaghetti and Meatball."

He laughs. "Yeah. That was kinda sad."

"Yeah."

"And then remember you rode your bike off the sidewalk and you yelled 'ow'?"

"Yup. I remember."

"And I *told* you, that doesn't even hurt.

He pronounces the word hurt like "Hoyt."

"It hurt *me*! Maybe it hurts girls. It hurt my vagina."

And he threw his head back laughing with his mouth open so wide that I could see all of his teeth.

Then he changed the subject, declaring: "Rice Krispie Treats that you buy at the store are dumb," and we did not mention the leaving thing again.

On the way to the airport, I stared out the window, while Henri's mom, my aunt, drove her Jaguar. I remembered the time that Henri was so angry with me that he slammed the door in my face and screamed, "I'm not gonna love you *ever*!" because I'd given him an Altoid that was too spicy.

I started feeling guilty about my year of babysitting. I felt I could have done a better job. I could have been more patient. More kind.

"I'll never be a good mom," I blurted out to my aunt, choking up. As soon as I said it, I realized that it was a fear of mine, one I'd never admitted to anyone before.

My aunt shook her head.

"Oh, Chloe," she said. "That's not true. You know what you did? You talked to them like they were real people. Like they were your peers. You respected them. Even moms have days where they want to lock themselves in the bathroom."

At the airport, I studied the screen that listed the departures. I looked at the familiar ones: New York City. Berlin. Seattle. I looked at the ones that were exotic to me, that still gave me a flutter in my stomach. Chicago. Honolulu. Paris. The places I could go. Where would I end up?

Just before I went through security, I knelt down and cupped Henri's worried face in my hands and asked him if he knew how much I loved him. "Duh," he said, smiling. "True love," he said. And he threw his little arms and legs around me like a monkey.

Which makes me think I have done well in the realm of love—that I have progressed. Because I think if you tell someone that you love him or her, (especially a person that once screamed, "I'm not gonna love you *ever!*") and that person says "duh," then I think that means you have done something right. I felt happy about "duh." I felt even better about "true love," which, believe it or not, is not a term he got from me. But he's been throwing it around. I don't know where he got it—maybe from pre-school.

I felt okay about love while I walked down the ramp to the airplane that would bring me home.

Thank you to the editors of the following journals, where these essays have appeared in a slightly different form:

SMITH, Volume 1 Brooklyn, Freerange Non-fiction, Mr. Beller's Neighborhood, The Frisky, Used Furniture Review, Gloom Cupboard, Jersey Devil Press, Connotation Press, PANK, Awosting Alchemy, Smalldoggies, The Nervous Breakdown, The Faster Times, Everyday Genius, and *LUMINA.*

Chloe Caldwell lives in New York. This is her first book.

Visit her at www.chloecaldwell.com

ACKNOWLEDGMENTS

Many people shared with me the joy, tears, and headaches that went into this book. I cannot name them all but I would like to thank the below people for their efforts.

My father for being one-hundred percent full of support, every hour of every day, for giving me a desk and a door, and for always accepting my passions with a vengeance.

My mother for her endless encouragement, and for showing me just how tremendously one person can love another.

Trevor Caldwell for telling me that it seemed like I wanted to be a writer.

Eric Wybenga, thank you for your eyes, for doing the dirty work, (and there was a lot of it) always with such good humor and anal-retentiveness.

Bryan Coffelt for creating this beautiful book design, his efficiency, and dedication.

Sean H. Doyle for reminding me to keep my head down and do the work, and for always being there there to read it when it was done. Thank you for being such a friend on the dark days and the bright.

Aaron DiMunno, who was my audience of one for many years, and who shared with me the urge to indulge in the inexplicable beauty of writing.

My ridiculously supportive friends: Hannah Calhoun, Ashlee Alamillo, Noelle Bruneau, Skye Tyler, Nat Gelb, and Michael Juliani.

Special thanks to Lidia Yuknavitch, Elizabeth Ellen, Poe Ballantine, and Molly Oswaks.

My Portland family, who welcomed me into their homes with open arms: Dena Rash Guzman, Amy Temple Harper, B. Frayn Masters, Jessie Carver, and Nora Robertson.

My amazing Seattle family: The Quigley-Isaacson's.

Eternal graciousness and love to Cheryl Strayed, who I was fortunate to have as an encouraging mentor and generous friend, and who told me to keep on writing like a mother-fucker. Thank you, Cheryl.

My remarkable teachers at the *Gotham Writers Workshop*: Sarah Grace McCandless, Katherine Dykstra, Cheryl Burke, (Rest in Peace) and Melissa Febos.

Thank you to the influential and inspiring, always legendary and never forgotten, Jack Young, Jr.

And lastly, the extraordinary Kevin Sampsell. Thank you for believing in my writing enough to put it in print. Thank you for your tireless patience and profound compassion, and for being fiercely loyal to this book. Thank you from the depths of my heart.

To all of my other dear family, friends, and readers: Thank you. My love for you is enormous.

ALSO AVAILABLE FROM FUTURE TENSE BOOKS:

I Remember by Shane Allison

Wish You Were Me by Myriam Gurba

The Book of Freaks by Jamie Iredell

Ventriloquism by Prathna Lor

OK, Goodnight by Zachary Schomburg and Emily Kendal Frey

Put Your Head in My Lap by Claudia Smith

Everything Was Fine Until Whatever by Chelsea Martin

Partial List of People to Bleach by Gary Lutz

To order any of these books, or for more information about the press, visit www.futuretensebooks.com.

Most Future Tense Titles are available through Small Press Distribution.

CPSIA information can be obtained at www.ICGtesting.com
Printed in the USA
LVOW130551230512

282931LV00003B/1/P

9 781892 061423